TOGETHER
ON THE ROAD
Priesthood, today and tomorrow

Massimo Camisasca
Together on the Road
Priesthood, today and tomorrow

Translated by Michelle K. Borras
Edited by Jonah Lynch

FRATERNITY OF ST. CHARLES
Passion for the glory of Christ

Book design by Melissa Galliani
cover photo: Martin Fisch

ISBN: 978-0-9823561-2-8

Massimo Camisasca

TOGETHER
ON THE ROAD
Priesthood, today and tomorrow

Contents

Foreword

Since the first Christians fled the decadent urban environment of late antiquity to populate the inhospitable desert areas of the East, God has ensured that a form of Gospel living exists to suit the particular needs of each generation. Because the Church is understood as the Body of Christ, comprised of Head and members, these ecclesial forms always embody some variety of communion among persons: companies, monasteries, convents, fraternities. It belongs to the nature of the Church to generate new forms of living together. There is nothing odd about the notion of ecclesial communion. From the time that Christ called his first apostles, Christian consecration has always entailed persons living together, whether in a family, in a monastery, or–in the case of diocesan priests–in a presbyterate.

As a Franciscan, I recall how the rise of the Mendicant Friars in the early thirteenth century illustrates this claim about *communio*. St. Francis of Assisi recognized the need for a transnational brotherhood that would follow the Gospel commandments without compromise. In an age when the structures of mercantilism began to dominate the lives of ordinary Christians, including arguably the saint's own father, the Poor Man of Assisi urged his followers to observe a radicalism that strove to imitate that of the Savior himself. Lady Poverty became the mistress of Francis Bernadone. God both authenticated and rewarded this radical embrace of the Gospel when he imprinted on the body of Saint Francis the same wounds that the Savior himself had endured for our salvation.

At the start of the twenty-first century, divine Providence continues to provide new forms of Christian life and renewal. One expression of this provident and generous divine action is found in what the Church calls ecclesial movements. Like all Christians, those who associate themselves with these "new movements" commit themselves to enacting some form of *communio*. Their form of living together, however, differs from what transpires within the older forms: The companies of desert hermits, the monasteries of monks, the convents of nuns, and the friaries of friars. Their communion develops in a way particularly suited to the needs of our contemporaries. In order to learn what distinguishes the fraternities associated with the "new movements" from other forms of intense Christian living, we need to discover the experiences of those whom God has made the special instruments of their establishment. We must listen to the voices of the new founders and of those who have inspired them.

To introduce one of these voices is now my privilege. It is that of the Italian priest Massimo Camisasca, a figure of the post-Conciliar period who has been instrumental in developing new forms of living together. Specifically, I have been asked to introduce his book, *Together on the Road*. As the title suggests, Monsignor Massimo Camisasca has taken up in our own day the imperatives of divine Providence by describing a new form of being together. His program particularly suits the international dimensions that the Church has attained at the dawn of the twenty-first century, and which requires worldwide mobility–being on the road.

Together on the Road explains the inspiration behind a new group of priests whose *communio* finds its centering point not in a monastery or in a friary, but in a "house." The Priestly Fraternity of the Missionaries of St. Charles Borromeo represents one of the many new forms of Gospel life that have grown up in the Church since the close of the Second Vatican Council. This year marks the fortieth anniversary of the Council's solemn closing. At the same time, we observe the twentieth anniversary of the inauguration of this priestly fraternity that developed out of a deep and Christian experience of friendship among several young priests. That they chose as their patron the saintly sixteenth-century Bishop of Milan reflects not only their geographical homelands, but also their identification with the renewal of Catholic life that took place during the sixteenth century after the Council of Trent. The noble-born Charles Borromeo was one of the architects of what is now called the Catholic Reform.

Massimo Camisasca himself was born in Milan shortly after the end of the Second World War. While a high school student at the Liceo Berchet, the young Massimo met a priest of extraordinary grace and intelligence. Don Luigi Giussani is the acknowledged founder of the ecclesial movement Communion and Liberation, whose members dedicate themselves to an intense form of Christian witness and presence in many different venues. Since he has become a revered teacher in the Church, the name of Don Giussani inspires countless Catholics all over the world[1].

---

[1] Luigi Giussani was born in 1922 in Desio, a small town near Milan, Italy. At a very young age he entered the diocesan seminary of Milan, continuing his studies and finally completing them at the theological school of

The secularization of Western culture that we in the United States have come to confront dramatically over the past thirty years or so, finds its proximate origins in the upheavals throughout Europe that followed the end of the Second World War. When in 1960 the young fourteen-old Massimo Camisasca met Don Luigi Giussani, this precocious adolescent discovered a form of Christian life that has shaped his personal development in the faith and guided his own unique form of apostolic outreach. That leadership would befall the future Don Massimo was apparent early on, from the time when he was given responsibility for Communion and Liberation's Student Youth Movement, *Gioventù Studentesca*,[2] and subsequently became one of the main leaders of the Communion and Liberation Movement itself.

The Priestly Fraternity of St. Charles Borromeo grew out of the fraternal and missionary spirit that animated a group of priests who, while still in the seminary, had been influenced by the writings of Don Giussani. Don Massimo became their leader, although as our author himself observes, he never foresaw or planned for this development. Once again, we see the workings of divine provi-

---

Venegono. After ordination, Fr. Giussani devoted himself to teaching at the seminary in Venegono (particularly Eastern theology, especially the Slavophiles, American Protestant theology, and Fundamental Theology). In 1954 he left the seminary and, from 1954—1964, taught at the Berchet classical high school in Milan. From 1964—1990 he occupied the chair of Introductory Theology at the Università Cattolica del Sacro Cuore in Milan. In 1954, Luigi Giussani's experience of faith gave rise to the movement Communion and Liberation, now present in over sixty-three countries. Fr Giussani died on February 22, 2005, in Milan.

[2] "Student Youth," the original nucleus of a group of Catholic high school and university students animated by Fr. Giussani, which would eventually develop into the movement Communion and Liberation. [—Tr.]

dence that proceeds sweetly but firmly. The Holy See recognized in 1999 this institute of missionary priesthood as a Society of Apostolic Life, and so gave to its members—140 of them—the freedom to pursue their mission and vocation wherever the Church most needs their distinctive style of Gospel living and preaching: Together on the Road!

I invite all who take up this little book to read it attentively. You will find in these pages a glimpse of how God raises up in the Church of Christ new forms of priestly life and ministry. Even if one is not in a position to respond to a priestly vocation, the attentive reader will discover in these pages a rich instruction in what it means to be Catholic today. The word "catholic" means universal, according to the whole. Rank individualism and the personal isolation that accompanies an attachment to "doing it alone" never characterizes authentic Gospel living. St. Francis of Assisi urged the necessity of communion in the thirteenth century. Massimo Camisasca has become a teacher of the same mystery in our own period. His experience merits and will repay the time that one spends discovering what is unique about Monsignor Camisasca's effort at keeping alive a living memory of Christ.

Seán Patrick O'Malley, O. F. M. Cap.
Archbishop of Boston

Preface to the American Edition

Although I never foresaw or planned it, for the last eighteen years I have dedicated myself to the formation of young seminarians who, once ordained priests, enter a fraternal community of missionary priests that I founded and currently serve as superior.

The name of this community is the Priestly Fraternity of the Missionaries of St. Charles Borromeo. It started in 1985 within the friendship of several young priests who had been living as brothers since their seminary days. This fraternal experience arose from their shared and ever-deepening belonging to the movement of Communion and Liberation.

These priests recognized their friendship as an authentic fruit of belonging together and at the same time an adequate form of the mission to which the Lord had called them. From its beginning, the Fraternity has been characterized by community, life, and mission.

A witness to Christ happens where one walks together with others. For this reason we in the Fraternity go together in mission and live together in houses. The house is the privileged support for our vocation, an experience of pardon and correction, and the most immediate aid in living the memory of Christ.

We go in mission moved by the desire that Christ be known in the fascinating way which attracted and convinced us. Materially, that means we go where bishops invite us or permit our presence both in order to evangelize and to sustain or begin a presence of the movement of Communion and Liberation. The Fraternity is the mission of Christ to every person, that wherever the possibility is open, this mission may occur.

We have also chosen to remain in countries where ancient local churches with rich traditions are going through the crisis of secularization. We wish to be missionaries according to the vision the Church has always had of them throughout its 2,000 year history: men and women who announce Christ, because "there is no other name under heaven given among mortals by which we must be saved" (Acts 4:12)

Our members are now present in twentyfor houses in seventeen countries, from the United States to Siberia, Europe to South America, Kenya, and Taiwan.

These pages are dedicated to them and to whoever desires to meet us and get to know us; and more generally to anyone thoughtful about the truth and vitality of priesthood. Must I add that this is not a short essay, nor a formative guide, nor a history? This is simply the echo of a gift received.

I
The Church's Mission

For How Long?

Even the person aware that the Christian faith will always be the object of contradiction and active resistance cannot but feel challenged at the present moment, as the Church is experiencing a very visible attack from fundamentalism on the one hand, and a more subtle and profound attack from other powers on the other. As almost every day brings new massacres and new martyrs, the question arises in us: for how long?[3] Chapter six of the Book of the Prophet Isaiah, in which we find precisely this disconsolate question, comes to mind.

The chapter opens in a presentation of two great realities, which are strictly joined: vocation and mission (Is 6:1-9). The prophet has a marvelous experience of God, full of light and wonder, but also of dismay at his littleness in the face of such grandeur. Through the power of this meeting, Isaiah is made suddenly conscious of his misery, which corresponds to a perception of impurity and unease. But the prophet's conclusion is surprising. He says, "My eyes

---

[3] Between 2000-2004, there were 140 missionaries—priests, religious and lay persons—killed throughout the world (information from the Vatican's Martyrology of the Church published by the Pontifical Congregation for the Evangelization of Peoples, available online at www.fides.org).

have seen the King, the LORD of hosts" (Is 6:5), and the reality of this meeting is more real than all of his weakness. He realizes that he has been purified. A new way of looking at life takes shape in him, and his heart is lit up to love truly.

Just at that moment a voice is heard: "Who will go for us?" (Is 6:8). God calls for one reason: to make himself known. Isaiah, who is called, understands that the experience of God is for a mission and responds, "Here am I! Send me!" (Is 6:8). The mission involved is delicate and difficult: the prophet will speak, but will not be understood, and when he tells people to look at what is happening with their own eyes, they will not see.

"Make the mind of this people dull, and stop their ears, and shut their eyes, so that they may look with their eyes, and listen with thier ears, and comprehend with their minds" (Is 6:10). These words, which conclude the revelation to Isaiah in the Temple and are taken up repeatedly by Jesus in the Gospels, show that the people will turn to the Lord only from the depths of betrayal. The action of mercy passes through the incomprehensibility and the hardness of refusal. The prophet, realizing both the bitterness and the positive aim of his mission, asks, "How long, O Lord?" (Is 6:11). Will all this hardness have a result? Will there be a change, a healing? God answers:

"Until the cities lie waste without inhabitant, and houses without people, and the land is utterly desolate; until the LORD send everyone far away, and in the midst of the land. Even if vast in the emptiness a tenth remain in it, it will be burned again, like a terebinth or an oak whose stump remains standing when it is felled". The holy seed is its stump (Is 6:11-13).

I think that this passage brings to light a great rule for every Christian missionary vocation: the missionary does not have to be preoccupied with the number of persons that can be reached or who will respond, but rather with the truth of the experience that he or she proposes in its *essentiality* and *depth*. These are the characteristics of the "holy seed" God speaks of to Isaiah.

Essentiality, or being preoccupied with all that is necessary— and only that which is necessary— to the life of the person. The "holy seed" appears as a barren stump, without leaves or fruit; the leaves and fruit will come when God wills it, but everything must be absolutely centered on what really matters (cf. Mt 10:9-10).

Depth, because the stump is ready to renew the tree from the roots and, to quote the poet Clemente Rebora, to "strike root in the truest place."[4]

Sheep Without a Shepherd

Two thousand years ago, the Father sent his Son into the world; the Son in turn wished to send the apostles, and others together with them. Why? First of all, because he had compassion on human beings.

We see in our time, as in perhaps no other epoch of history, the truth of Jesus' words when he compared people, worn out from the lack of guidance, to sheep without a shepherd (cf. Mt 9:36-38). The sheep wander about in search of grass that can satisfy their hunger and water that can

---

[4]   C. Rebora, "Il pioppo," in *Le poesie*, (Milan: Garzanti, 1994), 297.

quench their thirst, but, since they are not guided, they often travel along paths where the grass is scorched, paths that do not lead to refreshing streams. They move in circles, along ways that lead nowhere, and finally tire out, fall, and despair.

The glory of Christ is his passion for the human person; our missionary life, too—as Christians, as priests—is part of this passion. But one cannot be sent or go forth without having been constituted. One cannot be fruitful without being continually rooted in the tree that is the Church, i. e., without a living, conscious, active, and passionate belonging to the Church. Not a single one of us has been chosen because of merit. Rather, each has been chosen for a purpose and is continually being filled with gifts, which are granted in order to be given away. We are called in order to be filled with something that does not come from us, and that does not belong to us. This is the only foundation of our right and authority.

When I read chapter 10 of the Gospel of Matthew, I am struck to discover that Jesus, when he explains what will happen after him, sees the whole history of the Church as in a flash of premonition: the history of the persecutions and opposition that she will have to suffer (cf. Mt 10:22-42). Jesus knows perfectly what happens and what will happen to us. We must be conscious of this and prepare ourselves for it, but we have the certainty that everything we will have to say will be suggested to us by him. The truer a mission is, the more it will unleash the hatred of the devil; divisions will take place even within families. Those enslaved by the Prince of Lies will oppose the person who lives in truth. We must always remember that, as Jesus said, we will be hated for his name's sake, so that we do not tremble in the face of difficulties, in those moments when people abandon us, or because of subtle or even blatant opposition.

Jesus is a sign of contradiction. He does not want division, but division is necessarily provoked by the choice he demands[5]. The worst thing for a missionary is to fail to recognize the confidence that Jesus brings into our lives, and thus to live in an exaggerated fear, even to the point of failing to see the nearness of Jesus and of the other. We are dear to Jesus. He, who is one with the Creator, loves every detail of our lives and persons. He loves us within our personalities. We must, then, recognize Jesus and declare ourselves for him, even if this costs us the most difficult divisions from those most dear to us.

The last verses of Matthew, chapter 10, are full of consolation and light. They speak of our identification with Jesus and of the recompense that will be given to us if we believe in God's justice, if we give ourselves completely to those whom we wish to make into Jesus' disciples. All the more will we receive the promised reward: "And whoever gives even a cup of cold water to one of these little ones in the name of a disciple truly, I tell you, none of these will lose theri reward" (Mt 10:42). Each one of us is one of these "little ones." That is the phrase Jesus uses to describe his disciples, so that it might shed its light over our whole existence and vocation.

Taking up the Cross

"Whoever does not take up the cross and follow me is not worthy of me. Those who find their life will lose it" (Mt

---

[5]   Cf. *La Bibbia di Gerusalemme* (EDB, Bologna 1990, 2108) (n. to Mt 10:34).

10:38-39). A more interesting translation of verse 39, "he who wishes to save his life will lose it," points us to Paul's Letter to the Philippians, in which the apostle reminds us that Jesus kept nothing for himself (cf. Phil 2:6-8). We, too, must keep nothing for ourselves, because "we do not live to ourselves, and we do not die to ourselves" (Rom 14:7); rather, we must "take up the cross" (Mt 10:38).

I have always wondered what "take up the cross" meant for Jesus before he was crucified. Then I discovered that this was a common expression in ancient Aramaic, and I found an interesting comment in a book by a Protestant exegete:

Detachment from oneself and the gift of oneself to God have an extreme measure. In life, there is a limit from which one can clearly see if the dedication is entirely willed. This limit is death. The person who, in the risk of choosing God, includes also the possibility of losing his earthly life, has truly decided in a radical way. Only when the disciple has calculated and consciously accepted even this extreme possibility, is he truly a disciple of the Master and worthy of him. Not every disciple is asked to demonstrate this disposition by actually being killed. But every gift of self—and this is the theme and meaning of our life— already contains something of this dying. A sure measure of the truth of our sentiment is whether or not we are prepared also for this.[6]

---

[6] W. Trilling, *Vangelo secondo Matteo* (vol. 1) (Rome: Città Nuova 1975), 209.

The Church celebrates the cross of Christ in festive tones: *"Crux fidelis, inter omnes / arbor una nobilis: / nulla silva talem profert, / fronde, flore, germine"* ("O faithful cross, noblest of trees: no glade contains its equal in branches, roots, and flowers").[7] Is it not a contradiction to speak of the "exaltation" of the cross? Isn't this sort of language far removed from us and our lives? Isn't it almost sarcastic and sacrilegious to speak of glory and joy in reference to the most horrible instrument of torture and execution that history records? Isn't it a complete contradiction to speak of the death of God, of the end of the one who had come to reign and to save all men and women from death?

The cross is the condition for life and for glory. Our poor concepts and narrow parameters must be exploded to make room for an event that is new, unimaginable, but which nevertheless happened: the merciful love of God for each one of us. The cross—that is, the recognition of the Father, of his will, of his plan made manifest in Jesus—is the path of glory. *"O crux, ave, spes unica! / in hac triumphi gloria / piis adauge gratiam / reisque dele crimina"* ("Hail, O cross, only hope! In the glory of this triumph increase your grace in those who trust in you, cancel the guilt of us sinners").[8] In accepting and experiencing passion and death, Christ received from the Father the gift of being lifted up above all things forever, as the beginning and first-born of the definitive world. So we understand how the cross is both necessary and relevant. Even more, we see the expectation for

---

[7] Traditional hymn for Good Friday, text taken from *Canti* (Milan: Cooperativa Editoriale Nuovo Mondo, 1995), 29.

[8] From the hymn *"Vexilla Regis,"* taken from the liturgy of the Hours.

it in people who do not know how to see and yet, even in their distance and with their refusal, express an unconscious thirst for God.

Priests: Friends and Servants

He made himself obedient, even a servant (cf. Phil 2:7-8). Here is the heart of the priestly ministry: servants of Christ and therefore servants of members of the human community. We are servants because we are called to be the custodians and distributors of a good that is not ours. But we are also friends because we have been introduced, through the ministry entrusted to us, the knowledge of everything: "I have called you friends, because I have made known to you everything that i have heard from my Father" (cf. Jn 15:15). Could there be a greater and more inexhaustible intimacy?

The priesthood is a privileged form of Christ's presence here and now, at the side of each person.[9] If Christ were simply a man of the past, however fascinating he might be, what importance would he have for us? The richness of his experience or his knowledge, the works he performed, might interest us at most like the deeds of great men and women recorded in history books. But he is not just a man who lived an extraordinary experience or who showed an exceptional humanity, generating a following that has not been interrupted for 2,000 years. He is alive, present, here among us; his words are addressed to us and touch us as

---

[9] The use of "privileged" to refer to the priesthood, both here and further on in the thext, should not be misinterpreted in terms of power, but rather, understood within the framework of friendship and service.

no one else's words can. In Jesus Christ is united the exceptional nature of a human experience with its permanence in time.

The one who follows Christ as a priest has not only heard his voice as something present, his proposal as more pertinent to life than any other. Through the attraction of Christ's person, he has desired to place himself entirely at the service of the Lord's contemporaneity.

There are many ways to follow Christ, but one of fundamental importance is certainly that which the Lord himself established: the proclamation of his presence, the gift of the sacraments, the ministry that impresses on the priest an indelible seal which makes him a preeminent servant of Christ's mercy for human beings. To speak of him, to forgive sins, to make present the mystery of his body and blood in the sacrament of the Eucharist, to educate the Christian people: what is greater than being able to serve Christ in these tasks? It is a privileged way of being by his side, of being useful to him, of being loved by him and of loving him in each human being. The priest draws the strength of his mission from the mystery of Jesus' personal predilection. If one day the priest feels tired, lonely, contradicted, forgotten, or persecuted, he should remember that it is not because Christ is far away, but because he is particularly near and wants him to share so much in his solitude and passion that he generates its permanence in history.

The stupendous mosaic that can be admired in the apse of the Basilica of St. Clement in Rome unites the triumph of the cross and the life of the Church. There, it is clear that the cross is not a sign of death, but of life; it is not a sign of the end, but of glory. It gives rise to the Gospel, symbolized by the four evangelists at its feet; the Church is born in the encounter between the Old and New Testaments, represented by Saints Peter, Clement, Jerome, Paul, Laurence, and Isaiah. Bethlehem is joined to Jerusalem, because, in the Incarnation, the new and definitive people is born in which the ancient people continues and finds its fulfillment. The hand of God places the wreath of triumph on the cross, from which twelve doves arise and descend, representing the twelve apostles, with Mary and John on the sides. The mosaic describes the whole history of the world, within which is inserted the history of every generation of the Christian people.

The Place of a True Humanity

We have an immense responsibility in the circumstances in which we find ourselves living, in an age in which the "desertification" of the world, through the acceleration of historical processes, can be seen from day to day. A few examples: it is self-evident that a child has the right to a stable family and that no one can demand to have a child, but ideologies have erected immense walls in the face of this evidence and created a vast distance from it. It is as if those who recognize the evidence found themselves on small oases in the desert, miniscule communities in a desolate land, microscopic lights in an immense darkness. We must recognize this as the plan of God in the present moment of the history of the world. What a huge and fascinating responsibility is given to us! But also what a necessity to be true, serious, total!

The core of Christianity, or rather the heart of existence, is in fact very simple. The truth of life is implicated in the phrase, "Unless you become like children..." (Mt

18:3). The experience of the child consists in recognizing what is in front of him or her, in accepting the need for help in life, in acknowledging the need for another who leads the child to him or herself. No one can save oneself (and here we see the lie behind the "New Age" movement).

The difficulty in speaking to people today is also tied to the fact that, in the course of a very brief period of time, the same words no longer mean the same things; they do not even contain an experience analogous to that which they might have had thirty years ago. This is a sign of the penetration of power, as then Cardinal Joseph Ratzinger observes in his book-length interview, *Salt of the Earth*:

> The danger of a dictatorship of opinion is growing, and anyone who doesn't share the prevailing opinion is excluded, so that even good people no longer dare to stand by such nonconformists. Any future anti-Christian dictatorship would probably be much more subtle than anything we have known until now. It will appear to be friendly to religion, but on the condition that its own models of behavior and thinking not be called into question.[10]

Our path to Christ cannot do away with the context in which he places his Church today; it cannot avoid the troubled waters through which she has to pass (and thus also ourselves). It is impossible to separate election from responsibility, but responsibility and response cannot

---

[10] J. Ratzinger, *Salt of the Earth: Christianity and the Catholic Church at the End of the Millenium*, trans. Adrian Walker, (San Francisco: Ignatius Press, 1997), 153.

exist except in an awareness of the historical moment in which Christ has called us to live. We cannot think that our mission will unfold, for example, in a context like that of the Middle Ages or of the seventeenth century; we live in an age marked by the crumbling of the historical presence of the Church. Ratzinger explains,

> At present, Christianity is suffering an enormous loss of meaning, and the form in which the Church is present is also changing. The Christian society that has existed until now is very obviously crumbling. In this respect, the relationship between the society and the Church will also continue to change, and it will presumably continue in the direction of a dechristianized form of society. What is happening in the world of faith will no longer automatically have an innovative impact on the general conscious-ness of society.[11]

Many purveyors of opinion note that democracies are now in crisis. But democracy arises as responsibility in persons who are aware of being the voice of a people. Today the pyramid is upside down:

> The central area of life today is that of economic and technical innovations. There—and, in a very special way, in the entertainment world of the media as well—language and behavior are shaped. That is, as it were, the central zone that is addressed in great mass movements. In this case, religion hasn't disap-

---

[11] Ibid., 126.

peared, to be sure, but it has migrated into the realm of subjectivity. Faith is then tolerated as one of the subjective forms of religion, or else it retains a certain space ultimately as a cultural factor. On the other side, however, Christianity will offer models of life in new ways and will once again present itself in the wasteland of technological existence as a place of true humanity. That is already happening now.... In [the ecclesial movements], Christianity is present as an experience of newness and is suddenly felt by people—who often come from very far outside—as a chance to live in this century. Hence the public function of the Church will no longer be the same as it was with the traditional fusion of Church and society, but it will still be visible, even publicly, as a new opportunity for man.[12]

God has called us to a great task: responding to the urgent need for the humanity of Christ to continue to provoke human beings, so that the Christian people might continue to exist. The awareness of the historical task which God has given to us can lend gusto to every moment of our lives. It is essential, however, as we learn from Isaiah, that whatever we say comes from an experience, first of all in ourselves. A people is not an abstraction, but an "accumulation" of persons united by a presence. "Accumulation" means that everyone is included: the young with their clarity and enthusiasm, the elderly with their weariness and perhaps even disillusionment: our moments of exaltation and our sins, our greatness and our limitations. A people

---

[12] Ibid., 126-127.

is a mixture of flesh and spirit, carnality and transparency, good and evil. That which makes the unity of a people is not the absence of contradictions, but the finalization of every contradiction in a single end. Christ calls to our lives through everything that happens; we cannot choose what we will learn from, since God educates us even through evil.

The Church is probably heading toward an age of martyrdom, exclusion, or reduction. Precisely now, however, Christ gives the Church the gift of the ecclesial movements, of friendship, which teaches one how to be and how to generate a people. Our awareness of the greatness of the work to which we are called helps us to make our days tireless, really transforming them into work, moment by moment. To work is to ask that every circumstance, through the education of a people and through the education of one's own person, be an occasion of the revelation of the glory of Christ. In this way we understand the importance of study, silence, and every word that we hear, the preciousness of every call. St. Paul's urgency—"time has grown short" (1 Cor 7:29)—resounds in our time with a clamorous absoluteness. We recognize the importance of not wasting what is given to us and, at the same time, of not losing heart. Fatigue, weariness, and sadness can happen; they do and always will happen, but the knowledge of the tirelessness of our origin allows us continually to get up again. It is this that Sören Kirkegaard identified as the stuff of the mature life.[13]

---

[13] Cf. S. Kirkegaard, *La ripresa*, (Milan: Edizioni di Comunità, 1971).

The Necessity of Reform

Now more than ever, we must rediscover the relevance of the event of faith to human life. If Christian people lived centuries in which the faith was so alive that it determined the course of history, and further centuries of taking it for granted and forgetting, we live today in a time when people seem to be caught between two great alternatives. On the one hand, there is a fundamentalism that affirms faith by denying reason and ends in a destruction of the very possibility of the human person and God. It destroys the possibility of the human person, because the human being is thirst and expectation for an answer to the rational question about the meaning of life and reality, and it destroys the possibility of God, because the human person feels a natural repulsion for an image of God whose affirmation bases itself on the death of the questions posed by human reason. Rather, "faith is the recognition of an exceptional presence and adherence to what this presence says about itself…. Thus faith is rational, because it blossoms at the farthest limit of the dynamic of reason like a flower of grace, to which the person adheres with his freedom."[14]

The other attack which strikes deeply at the life of the Christian people has universal dimensions: it consists in the universalism of power, an empire that appears to have neither a geographical center nor visible leaders, but which profoundly determines the lives of peoples and individuals, creating zones of well-being and want, war and peace, life and death. This is especially visible in the capillary

---

[14] L. Giussani, "Il miracolo del cambiamento: Esercizi della Fraternità di Communione e Liberazione," supplement to the periodical *Tracce: Litterae Communionis*, a. XXV, n. 7 (July-August), 29-30.

nature of the penetration of the influence of the mass media and of information networks. When these are not truly used for humankind, they tend to palpably reduce the experience of freedom.

As Pope John Paul II observed on May 30, 1998, at the gathering for the International Encounter of the Ecclesial Movements in St. Peter's Square:

> In our world, often dominated by a secularized culture that foments and publicizes models of life without God, the faith of many is sorely tried, and is often suffocated or extinguished. We recognize, then, the urgent need for a strong proclamation and a solid and deep Christian formation... Here we have the movements and the new ecclesial communities: these are the response, prompted by the Holy Spirit, to the dramatic challenge of the end of the millennium. You are the response of providence.[15]

The Christian people has so often felt itself overpowered by the weight of its own sins, limits, and infidelity, by being profoundly attached, both internally and externally, to the mentality of the world and to worldly desires. And yet the Church is reborn in each instance, because the Beginning who is its origin willed to create ever-new forms of his permanence in the lives of those created in the image and likeness of God. "The Spirit makes the Church a river of new life that flows through human history."[16]

---

[15] John Paul II, "L'importanza dei carismi nella Chiesa," discourse delivered on the occasion of the encounter of the movements and new communities on May 30, 1998, in *La Traccia*, (Rome: IEI, 1998), 510/V, 7.

[16] Ibid., 509/V, 3.

Comforted by John Paul II's words, which moved us all, I see the gift of the Fraternity of St. Charles, to which I belong, as a tiny grain of sand on the shores of history, on the immense seashore that God promised to Abraham (cf. Gn 22:15-18).

The Apostolic Life

In the face of the enormous challenges that seem to strike at the heart of the very reality of the Christian people, as in a renewed struggle of David against the giant Goliath (cf. 1 Sam 17), the Church experiences several urgent needs. I would like to point out a few that I find particularly important.

Before all else, faith must once again become an experience capable of addressing all the dimensions of the human heart—an experience that convinces, because it responds to the intelligence and is creative on the level of the affections. As an educator of seminarians and priests my primary preoccupation is that of forming men who, with their humanity, engage the humanity of those who encounter them. Through the attraction of a different way of using reason and freedom, it is possible to explode the narrow horizons that the prevailing mentality forces onto the men and women of today.

Secondly, in the face of the greatness of such an undertaking, and in a society which divides each person from the other and from him or herself, Christians, and priests in particular, must have a fundamental experience of life in community. This represents the certainty that the real novelty that has come into the world is brought by God and not by human wisdom or intelligence (cf. 1 Cor 2:6). The wisdom of God is lived communion. This is why our community wanted to call itself a "fraternity," such an important word in the history of the Church (one thinks of St. Francis and St. Benedict). This word expresses the desire, within the uncertain and precarious hours of the present life, to beg for the experience of the life of the children of God the Father, given by the Spirit of God.

The priest's complete dependence on that which comes from God is expressed in the total dedication of his life to proclamation and to the celebration of the sacraments, to the gift of himself, of his time, his gifts and his energy, as the educator of the Christian people. But all this can come about only as the expression of a lived community. This is the reason why we decided to live in "houses," where each person can be the sign of the presence of Christ to the other and sustain his vocation. The Fraternity of St. Charles is a "society of apostolic life," the term used by the *Code of Canon Law*. This term also unites us to the life and times of the apostles, who left their goods and affections because they found in Christ a hundred times more than what they had left behind. They were brought together by him, lived with him, and then were sent into the whole world. In this going into the whole world, they retained an ideal and real reference to one another; they founded one thing only, the Church.

The third urgent need I would like to stress is that of mission. The Church must not let herself be tempted by the organizational and bureaucratic systems that the modern mindset tends to impose on it. Pope John Paul II tirelessly bore witness to the fact that Christians must never be afraid that Christ cannot be attractive for human beings. Christ is not a man of the past; he lives today and communicates himself with explosive energy. He is the *Word*.

Wherever our missionaries find themselves, I invite them constantly to remember what they *are*, in order then to *act* in truth. I am convinced that, today more than ever, the Church and the humanity to whom she is sent need men and women who are examples and witnesses to the "hundredfold" that is to be found in Christ the Redeemer (cf. Mt 19:29). Through this phenomenon of a changed humanity, Christ communicates himself to human beings.

There is a very thin line that separates the truth from lies; every experience, even the truest, must constantly be redeemed from the temptation to degenerate into activity and projects. It is Christ who saves; that which saves our lives, moment by moment, from the temptations that disfigure it, is the joy of living the Christian experience in our time. Nothing else interests us. Everything else is the superabundance of this.

II
A Priestly Fraternity

Vocation

In a conversation that took place many years ago, the philosopher Emmanuel Levinas said to me, "The human countenance is the place where, reciprocally for two people, the promise of God emerges: you will not die."[17] The promise of eternity is written on the faces of the people God places at our side; the face of the other is the sign that God gives to those he has created in his image to show them that they will not die. This reflection was the starting point for me from which I was able to recognize what had happened in my life. Through it, I recognized the method God used to form all my history and, through the circumstances, the history of the priestly fraternity I founded in 1985. To record this growth of the work of God in our midst is the only thing that matters—to recognize what God is doing and to adhere to it.

St. Augustine says that when we think we are seeking, it is we who are really sought; we cannot seek unless we have already been found. In every encounter or fact of life, there is always a "ruse," a sort of cunning on the part of God; through the concreteness of particular things (like the attractiveness of a gaze or a manner of speaking), God introduces us into a

---

[17] M. Camisasca, *Volti e incontri*, (Milan: Jaca Book, 1995), 61-62.

larger and ultimately absolutely unforeseeable dimension. The experience of every human being who knows that he or she is not the master of his or her life, and who does not position him or herself in reality with the goal of bending it to his or her will, consists in realizing that every relationship, with persons or with things, has a horizon that is greater than the immediacy or the instinctual nature of this here-and-now relationship. Something in it goes beyond the palpable aspects of reality. At first, the person intuits being pointed toward something much bigger, something that he or she does not quite manage to define. Then the person discovers that each moment and every aspect of a real experience leads along a path to the discovery of a beyond, a something greater.[18] Whoever has not at some point experienced this is living a lie by playing the role of the master of life.

Jesus promised St. Peter, "When you grow old, you will stretch out your hands, and someone else will fasten a belt around you and take you where you do not wish to go" (Jn 21:18). This experience of being led is a very concrete reality. We see it with our own eyes, step by step. Particularly when we look back on the steps already taken, we realize that events, circumstances, and conditions have led us in a precise direction. All of us think we are choosing our own path, but in reality we are being led all along. Although it may seem paradoxical, none of this takes anything away from our personal freedom; to the contrary, it is the realization of the person's freedom and truth. When someone realizes that the Lord is leading him or her, or even that he or she is being led by someone else through whom a glimpse of the Mystery is caught, this is not a negative experience of expropriation. That person finds him or her-

---

[18] Cf. L. Giussani, *Il senso religioso*, (Milan: Rizzoli, 1997), 64-67.

self brought to a greater breadth of life, to the only possibility of peace—which is the countenance of the people he or she meets, the people with whom he or she lives.

In one of the psalms, we read: "Great peace have those who love thy law; nothing can make them stumble" (Ps 119: 165). The law of the Lord, which makes those who receive it "happen," is not a stumbling block. God sends proofs into our lives. He does not cease to intervene in the concreteness of our life and to solicit our freedom. This freedom either recognizes or refuses him; what God gives becomes *dis*-grace when it is not recognized, and grace when it is received as an event to be followed.

Fraternity in the World

It is not at all common, at least in the Church, to draw a parallel between the fall of the Roman Empire and the historical moment we are currently living. In his interview, *Salt of the Earth*, Cardinal Ratzinger says,

> Perhaps the time has come to say farewell to the idea of traditionally Catholic cultures. Maybe we are facing a new and different kind of epoch in the Church's history, where Christianity will again be characterized more by the mustard seed, where it will exist in small, seemingly insignificant groups that nonetheless live an intensive struggle against evil and bring the good into the world—that let God in. I see that there is once more a great deal of activity of this kind.[19]

---

[19] J. Ratzinger, *Salt of the Earth*, 16.

Not long ago I heard Fr. Giussani cite a passage of Alasdair MacIntyre:

> A crucial turning point in that earlier history occurred when men and women of good will turned aside from the task of shoring up the Roman *imperium* and ceased to identify the continuation of civility and moral community with the maintenance of that *imperium*. What they set themselves to achieve instead—often not recognizing fully what they were doing—was the construction of new forms of community within which the moral life could be sustained so that both morality and civility might survive the coming ages of barbarism and darkness.[20]

This passage, written before the philosopher's conversion to Catholicism, can also serve as an introduction to my thoughts on the priesthood. It is from this perspective that I would like to speak of the priest and community among priests, free men who come together to help each other live out what has happened in their lives as the possibility for hope for every human being. It seems to me that the best historical example of this, though he is not explicitly mentioned in the quote from MacIntyre, is St. Benedict. Benedict's goal was neither to save the Roman Empire nor to create a Europe. He simply understood that the essence of Christianity lies in free persons who come together to give their whole lives for the sake of the truest thing that ever happened to them.

---

[20] A. MacIntyre, *After Virtue: A Study in Moral Theory* (Notre Dame, Ind: University of Notre Dame Press, 1981), 244.

The word "fraternity" describes the essence of the Christian event, and, for this reason, it can never be separated from the essence of the priestly life. It takes on a particular historical and existential importance particularly for the evil times in which we are called to live. All ages are ages of birth and death, and our age in particular is one of barbarity and darkness.[21] The faith today is rarely lived as an event; thus it can no longer shed light on the meaning of history or on the worth of the "I", i. e., the person as relation to the infinite in the present instant. We do not know how long this time of desolation will last. The Gospels reassure us in Jesus' eschatological discourses, "And if those days had not been cut short, no one would be saved; but for the sake of the elect those days will be cut short" (Mt 24:22), and "not a hair of your head will perish" (Lk 21:18).

Today more than ever, a vocation can be accompanied and sustained only in an experience of common life. The word "fraternity" (at least as much as the word "paternity") describes the fundamental characteristic of being, and in particular, of that Being which entered into history: the incarnate God, communion. "For in the one Spirit we were all baptized into one body—Jews or Greeks, slaves or free— and we were all made to drink of one Spirit" (cf. 1 Cor 12:13). The fruit of Baptism is a communion of life. So, too, everything that has its source in Baptism, like the priesthood, cannot but be an experience of communion, nourished by a fraternal community. In Christianity there is no call to a relationship with God that is not also an event of commun-

---

[21] "Barbarity and darkness" here is a theological verdict on the world's rejection of Christ, while still recognizing a present historical era marked by the evils of war, terrorism, rampant poverty, etc.

ion; there is no shortcut to God that bypasses Christ and his body. The problem of our times is precisely the spasmodic search for a shortcut to God (since the human person cannot do without God) which avoids the corporality of Christ.

Today, as in the beginning of Christian history, we can have the impression that we are tiny boats in the immense ocean of the world, flickering lights in the night. But these lights are fueled and these boats are sustained in their wanderings by an experience of friendship with God and with men and women. The paradigmatic point of this experience of friendship is surely the structure of silence that characterizes monastic communities; this should be a reference point even for the most difficult pastoral situations.

Silence and friendship are indivisible because a true gaze on the life of another person, one which recognizes and loves his or her destiny, can only exist in silence. This is not only a physical silence, but also a memory of the event that unites me to the other, and makes everyone one thing only. In certain moments of life, this experience of the unity realized in silence is very clear; it transfigures every detail of the day and of relationships, driving away banality, useless chatter, and division.

A community of people can be a light in the barbarity or darkness of the world, that world for which Christ died, only if it comes into existence through God's immense power. This is necessary so that the light might not be a candle whose flame is extinguished by the wind, or that the boat (an image of the Church that is often found in the Gospels) might not founder in the midst of storms and waves. This immense power of God builds us up in the silence of prayer and the sacraments that flow from Baptism.

The Origin and Face of the Priesthood

Baptism is the great event of our lives. The priesthood is called to serve Baptism, to serve the baptized and to serve human beings so that they might be baptized.[22] The priest has a special place that Christ has assigned to him within the community of the baptized. This is the meaning of our life in the world: to constantly propose the experience of baptism, an experience that can be had in every moment. In this sense, the vocation to the priesthood is at the same time a gift and a privilege. It is a gift that is grafted onto the gift of Baptism and grows as responsibility for the body of Christ, because without the ordained priesthood there is no Church, or at least, there is no orderly and fruitful growth of the Church. It is a privilege that is entirely exhausted in the service of Christ, in the service of the Church, in serving the people who believe and people so that they might believe. For this reason, St. Augustine said of himself, "With you I am a Christian, for you I am a bishop; the first is a joy, the second a responsibility."[23]

The priest's experience is one of being a man among men and women, through his condition of life, without seeking special privileges or exceptions for himself; through a passion for all that is human; through his capacity for listening, relationship, and forgiveness. The priest does not belong to a caste; he is conscious of having been from among others to be the sign of the newness of grace.

---

[22] When I speak of priesthood in these pages, I refer to the ordained priesthood (I do not make further mention of this so as not to burden the reader with repetition). Here in particular, I want to mention the unity between the ordained priesthood and the priesthood of all the baptized.

[23] Cf. St. Augustine, *Sermo* 340, 1: PL 38, 1438.

But he does not live an existence separate from others because he must be like Christ, who took upon himself the whole human condition. As St. Paul says, we are *baptized among the baptized*: "Not that we lord it over your faith; rather we are workers with you for your joy..." (2 Cor 1:24).

This immanence in the lives of others does not require anything special in order to be realized, but it can be beset by many dangers. For example, one can develop a way of living or exercising one's own authority that has become *routine*, almost a defense from the dramatic nature of every hour. It is easy to give an answer before listening to the question, to offer solutions "from on high" instead of helping them to flower from within the existence of those around us. It is easy to close oneself up in one's goods and commodities, in a possessive experience of relationships, money, or affections. It is easy to be afraid of trials, of the cross, and it is especially easy to turn communion into an instrument to be used.

Before being a man of God or a guide for the community, the priest is a *sign of Christ's mercy*; he is a man of God and a guide precisely as this sign of the mercy of God that is Christ. The priesthood is an assimilation to the life of Christ, to the person of Christ who is given to the human community. For this reason, the priest is, above all, the one who proclaims the event of faith. St. Paul's question, "How are they to believe in one of whom they have never heard?" (Rom 10:14) pinpoints the deepest level of the priestly experience, the level at which the person himself is at stake, notwithstanding his knowledge that the truth of the proclamation does not necessarily depend on the coherence of the herald. I think of the "whiskey priest" of Graham Greene's *The Power and the Glory*, or of Bernanos' *Diary of a Country Priest*, in which weakness becomes the only possible revelation of strength.

At the beginning of the Synod of Bishops dedicated to priestly formation, Ratzinger commented, "'Sacrament' means that I give something that I myself cannot give; I do something that does not depend on me; I am in a mission and have become the bearer of something which another has given to me."[24] The sacraments—in particular Baptism, Penance, and the Eucharist—assimilate the human being into Christ. They nourish and renew this assimilation, and thus they are the path to the world's authentic renewal, the way for the world to fulfill its destiny. *Deus innocentiae restitutor et amator* (God, restorer and lover of innocence).[25]

It seems to me that, especially in recent decades, the activism that has become fashionable in our churches, the clamorous search for organization, has almost drawn a veil over this total relativity of the priesthood to proclamation and the sacrament.

The relativity of the priesthood to Christ, and thus to the Church, can be expressed in the category of the servant, as this is presented to us in the Gospels. This category does not exhaust our relationship with Christ, but characterizes it. The word "friendship" indicates the trust with which Christ poured out his whole self into our lives: "I do not call you servants any longer, but I have called you friends" (Jn 15:15). But, as Augustine argues, the word "friend" alone does not sufficiently explain one's relationship with God: "Call me your friend; I will still consider myself your servant". Service is total availability for this friendship, and the word "servant" indicates that, within a person's availability for this unmerited intimacy, a differ-

---

[24] J. Ratzinger, *La Chiesa*, (Cinisello Balsamo, Milan: Paoline, 1991), 82.

[25] Collect of the Tuesday of the second week of Lent.

ence remains. In this sense, Christ's expression "useless servants" (Lk 17:10) is very eloquent: the servant is useless, not because what is done is of no importance, but because the reason for service is an availability to another who acts, the giving over of one's whole being to the One from whom everything comes.

A friendship that is lived without this attitude of total reference to Christ is a fiction, a lie that gives rise to serious delusions and terrible enmity. For example, it is impossible to make obedience depend on friendship: "I will obey you only if you are my friend." It may well be easier to obey when friendship is involved. For this reason, one hopes that friendship grows in the community, but one cannot say that obedience is possible only if the condition of friendship is met. We have to be aware that obedience is the path for our lives to be really assimilated to Christ's. This implies the experience of the cross—"My God, my God, why have you abandoned me?" (Ps 22:2)—and of the resurrection. Without this, our lives remain in a state of confusion and failure.

Priests of a Fraternal Association

The call to live the priestly vocation within a fraternal society is a great gift because it makes it easier to experience concretely the profound pedagogy of God and the Church. The diocesan priesthood should also be lived as a fraternal association or friendship, but this is more difficult to bring about.

Our total reference to Christ, our awareness of not lording it over others in faith, but of bearing only what has been given to us in our turn, can be expressed in the life of a fraternal communion in many ways: for example, in a great humility with respect to our brothers, in a great patience with respect to the times God has chosen for each one of us. In this way, we learn to be priests in the world; we learn to live with a great passion for the truth, for human destiny, and thus for the history of the world, for the battles that are fought between Good and Evil, God and Satan. Only by beginning with this awareness can we understand the meaning of the priest as a man of God and educator of the community.

The Priest: Man of God

Every Christian is called to live out a priesthood that he or she receives at Baptism, as St. Peter tells us: "Come to him, a living stone, though rejected by mortals yet chosen and precious in God's sight; and like living stones, let yourselves be built into a spiritual house, to be a holy priesthood, to offer spiritual sacrifices acceptable to God through Jesus Christ" (1 Pt 2:4-5). The human being is not a particle of dust floating abandoned in the universe. By absolute grace, he or she has received revelation, the knowledge of the meaning of everything, and has received this as fellowship offered to his or her own life; the relationship between the infinite made flesh and other human beings takes place insofar as the human person is called to become part of this mystery that reveals itself. The priest should also have this awareness, full of joy and wonder. More, he is called to ask for it every morning: "The offertory of the Mass is the culminating moment in which we enter into God's game with our own freedom. We say to him: All my life is yours, and so I cry to you, receive it, take it. Because we do not change our own lives; they are changed by the mystery of Christ at work in us."[26]

The priesthood is responsibility with respect to the world: *prophetic responsibility*, because the priest has a responsibility of proclamation; and *sacramental responsibility*, because he makes present the place where everything receives its worth, or better, because he makes it possible for each thing to acquire its meaning by becoming part of the body of Christ. In this perspective, the ordained priesthood is at the service of the priesthood of Christ: the expression of the Fathers, "everything that is taken up is healed,"[27] means that Christ's priesthood, communicated to us in Baptism through the bodily reality of the Church, allows each thing to receive its worth. In prayer, especially in the prayer of the breviary and in the celebration of the sacraments, the priest must be aware that through him, the voice of humanity becomes a cry to God, a supplication, an invocation, a request for forgiveness—so that people's questions, expectations, and begging are carried to the altar of God to become the Body and Blood of Christ. The priest gathers all prayers, spoken and unspoken, all the actions, expectations, questions and sacrifices of humanity. He is Moses, who held up his arms between heaven and earth, and Abraham, who begged God for salvation. The priest, as priest, is also called to a personal participation in Christ's sacrifice in an unforeseeable and ultimately mysterious manner.

The priesthood is a referential availability between heaven and earth, between God, human beings, and things; it anticipates the clarity with which we will one day

---

[26] L. Giussani, *Dalla liturgia vissuta: una testimonianza* (Milan: Jaca Book, 1991), 21.

[27] Cf. St. Athanasius, *Against the Arians*, 2, 70.

see all the invisible threads uniting existences and time. For this reason, the priesthood requires a total availability, of one's self, time, life. It requires virginity. Virginity is structural to the priesthood: only a total availability to Christ and to his brothers and sisters allows a man to work for the sake of the world's recapitulation in Christ. The Church has linked celibacy and the priesthood since the beginning; the person who interiorly accepts celibacy cannot view the priesthood as a profession or as the realization of a personal project. A priest is totally available to let his life become a collaboration with the priesthood of Christ, allowing Christ to carry his life in unforeseeable ways.

The Priest Creates a People

The place of the priesthood is not only the temple made of stones, but also, above all, the temple which is the body of Christ, God's dwelling place, the space of his presence in this world. The veil of the temple was torn asunder at Christ's death, and so the true and definitive temple is the body offered in sacrifice for us: "Sacrifices and offerings you have not desire, but a body you have prepared for me" (Heb 10:5). Augustine proclaims, "We render glory to God when we become the body of Christ."[28] In this sense, we understand what the priesthood of the faithful and the sacramental priesthood are. The ordained priesthood serves this formation of the Body of Christ; we glorify God by allowing ourselves be drawn into the act of love that was

---

[28] Cf. St. Augustine, The City of God, X, 6.

accomplished on the cross. And I,"when I am lifted up from the earth, will draw all people to myself" (Jn 12:32). The Eastern Church has an even more vivid sense than we of this cosmic nature of the liturgy, of the sacramental gesture.

The priesthood allows people to be reconciled: the priest is the *pontifex* ("bridge-builder"), the man of reconciliation, the man who creates the people because he allows forgiveness and received mercy to be present in its midst.

> In order for people to be able to be reconciled with one another, truly to forgive and bear with one another, [the priest] must help them to accept each other in diversity, to have patience with one another; he must be able to carry people in pain, in physical suffering, in delusions and humiliations, in the anguish that none of us is spared.[29]

The ability to carry pain is fundamental to being human, and the priest must learn this. If he does not, failure is inevitable; existence becomes anger, and the heart becomes arid.

Fidelity

Virginity means to look at each thing as a sign of Christ's presence.[30] In looking at the other's countenance, I recognize what God brings about and beg him to make this event a sign of the event of Christ. Then, whatever hap-

---

[29] J. Ratzinger, "*Prospettive della formazione sacerdotale oggi*," in *Mission et formation du prête* (Namur) 1990.

[30] Cf. L. Giussani, *Si può vivere così?* (Milan: Rizzoli, 1994), 349-354.

pens strengthens my certainty that the destiny of my life is good. This observation does not deny the moments in which the other's face is, or appears to be, the face of an enemy. Rather, it highlights the position with which we face others and the promise inherent in the faces of those who are near to us. Nonetheless, no face in a group of people is a promise if it does not make the others also into this promise. The reality that lies in a few faces makes all the other faces into a promise. God's promise is realized in time and allows the fellowship a continual passage from the reality of today to a new manifestation of the promise that is a greater reality, according to the boundaries that only God can establish for his work. It is impossible to be with others if we do not recognize the promise made to us in their faces, but we must constantly ask God that this really happen, so that he might guide us into the land we have not yet entered. All our life is a preparation for the present moment: even in the moment just before the decisive step across the Jordan, other faces represent our certainty of entering the Promised Land. They are the incessant demand that this happen for each and every one of us.

Now I understand very well that my whole life was a preparation for the Fraternity of St. Charles and that fidelity to life as vocation turns life into history. Maybe this cannot be understood at the beginning; one has to reach a certain age in order to realize that, in all the apparent zigzagging of one's life, a real history is taking shape. In this history, nothing is lost and everything is safeguarded. As Peter the Venerable wrote to Eloise of her beloved Abelard, "He is kept safe for you for eternity, so that he can be given back to you."[31]

---

[31] Cf. Abelard, *Lettere d'Amore di Abelardo e Eloisa*, (Milan: Garzanti, 1974), 431-432.

History has a secret, seemingly chance beginning, like the beginning of a growing seed, because the event of God among men and women always begins in the secret mystery of God's freedom. This is what happened in salvation history: through Mary's "Yes," God became flesh in her womb, "a clot of blood, something we might almost disregard, but real," as Fr. Giussani once said. Through her, this new life became an infant, an adolescent, someone to be followed, and, in the end, the Son became the faces of those who were his own: of John and all the others who were gathered around him in the Upper Room.

Each new step in human history, in the history of the event of each "I," is a new blossom, but on a trunk and on branches that already exist. Our faces, our awareness, our problems, and our discoveries are the flowering of the experience and the faces of those who came before us. Just as each new blossom does not cancel out a preceding spring but renews it, enriches it, makes it explode, our faces urge everyone to a new awareness.

Each new thing that is born is the way in which Christ teaches us, prompting us to take a step forward in our lives and in the lives of all. The greatest temptation is to resist new things. When we do this, it is as if we were scolding God for what he does. Each new thing that arises among us ought rather to oblige us to come out of ourselves, to rediscover that deep awareness of what has happened, which turns life into history.

History is the awareness of the unity of what appears to be disjointed; the historian is the person who knows how to probe the drama of freedom so deeply that he or she is able to grasp the unity of the apparently inorganic. Thus, life as history is the discovery of the realization of the promise, through a progressive flowering which both deepens what has happened in the past and unveils the present. And our love for those persons who have made this history is all the truer because we are aware that their faces were the certitude of the divine promise which is beginning to flower.

III
Living the Sacrament of the Other

One can speak of priestly fraternities or friendships in the Church from a juridical point of view.[32] This is an interesting approach, since law always reveals the history of humankind and sheds light on how the person has understood him or herself and others. Nevertheless, I would like to approach this topic from a more profound point of view, examining priestly fraternities or friendships as the expression of something essential to the life of the Church, and, even more fundamentally, to the human person as such. Our theme thus becomes the experience of friendship (obviously, we can cover only a few aspects of this experience here).

This existential approach to the theme of friendship is better suited to my own experience as the founder and superior of a priestly fraternity, a fraternity that has helped me to discover how much this friendship was an answer to my deepest desires, and also to the promise that the encounter with Christ had represented for my life.

Friendship in Antiquity

One gauge of the decisive importance of friendship in the life of the human community in every age is the fact that

---

[32] This essay reproduces a talk given in Rome to the school for priests of the Congregation for the Clergy, January 30, 2002.

humanity's greatest writers and philosophers have fre-
quently spoken of friendship, and have seen it as an essential key to understanding the human being as something
that enters into the very definition of life itself.

Among the many examples, I will cite only Aristotle and
Cicero. Aristotle, speaking of friendship in books eight and
nine of the *Nicomachean Ethics*, maintains "there is nothing
more necessary to life, and without it none of the goods is
good."[33] Cicero, in chapter six of his dialogue, *Lelius de
amicitia*, writes, "I know not whether, apart from wisdom,
there be anything better for man than friendship, the gift of
the immortal gods to his life."[34]

Friendship is thus seen by these great figures of pre-
Christian antiquity as a necessary good, a gift of God. It is
also considered to be the source of happiness. In chapter
27 of *Lelius*, for example, Cicero says that if charity and
benevolence—which, we shall see, are for him the characteristics of friendship—are eliminated from life, the possibility of joy is also eliminated.[35]

Friendship is thus an aspect of love. It is love's summit.
It involves, first of all, a reciprocity that is not necessarily
present in every love: one can love a thing, a good, and
even a person, without this love necessarily being harmed
by the absence of reciprocity. Friendship, on the other
hand, is an active virtue that implies the response of the
other: friendship implies a friend.

Even more, friendship implies that the friend is another
self (both Aristotle[36] and Cicero[37] say this), who is loved as

---

[33] Aristotle, *Nicomachean Ethics*, VIII, 1, 1155a.

[34] Cicero, *Lelius de amicitia*, VI, 20.

[35] Cf. Ibid., XXVII, 102.

[36] Cf. Aristotle, *Nicomachean Ethics*, IX, 4, 1166a.

[37] Cf. Cicero, *Lelius de amicitia*, XXI, 80.

one loves oneself. With a friend, one lives a life of concord and communion. The goods of the present life and those hoped for in the life to come all become an instrument for nourishing the harmony of this common life. Cicero defines friendship as *"consensio divinarum et humanum rerum"*—the convergence and common fruition of human and divine goods—lived *"cum benevolentia et caritate."*[38] The word "charity"—we note that with Cicero we are still outside a Christian context—bespeaks the gratuity that must be present in this convergence; the word "benevolence" bespeaks the desire that the sole measure of one's relationship with the other be the good of the other. One seeks no advantages in friendship—as we see in book 27 of *Lelius*—except those that flower of themselves within the friendship: the joy that arises from a life lived in wisdom and love.[39]

Aristotle adds an important note: friendship is active and selective, that is, it is nurtured by a preference. It is an intensity of love that turns life among friends into a school for the charity we are called to have for all.[40]

The Novelty Christ Brings into Relationships

At the high point of his life, Jesus, who had given ample testimony during his public life as to what friendship meant for him, chose some with whom he would have a closer relationship. Among the disciples he further chose that there be apostles, "that they might stay with him" (Mk 3:14), and to them he confided the whole mystery of his

---

[38] Cf. Ibid., XXVII, 102.
[39] Ibid.
[40] Cf. Aristotle, *Nicomachean Ethics*, VIII, 2, 1155b.

life. We see again the two characteristics of friendship already intuited by Cicero: community in human things and community in divine things. This community is the apostolic community, the highest example of friendship that history offers. It is Jesus himself who gives us the key to contemplating the experience he lived with his disciples: "I have called you friends, because I have made known to you everything I have heard from my Father" (Jn 15:15).

Christ lived this friendship as the culmination of the charity to which he gave birth in his incarnation, death, and resurrection; in order to understand what this friendship really is, then, we must participate in his life. The friendship that he lived with his most intimate companions, the friendship that he has made possible among human beings, is born today from his sacraments: from Baptism, Eucharist, and Penance. It is born also from his teaching. It manifests itself in his followers, in their recognition of the central place he asks to take in the lives of those who encounter him. Friendship with Christ is lived out as service to his person (Augustine rightly comments on the phrase from John cited above: "you call me friend, and I continue to consider myself your servant").

Precisely for this reason, many Christian thinkers have written very profoundly of friendship. Their reflections clarify and fulfill the intuitions of the ancient philosophers through their own personal experience of friendship lived in a Christian context (often a monastery). St. Thomas, for example, takes over many themes from both Cicero and Aristotle. For him, as for them, friendship is *"amor benevolentiae,"*[41] the love that wills the good of the other, a love of

---

[41] Thomas Aquinas, *Summa Theologiae* II, II, q. 25, a. 4.

community, of exchange, a love that consists in treating one's friend as oneself. Friendship rests upon a community of life, goods, and virtues. As the summit of charity, friendship grants a person the experience of the divine life. Is not the Trinity the highest and most unattainable example of friendship?

It is not by chance that Aelred of Rievaulx, another great medieval scholar of friendship (a category that includes Bernard), affirms in book two of his *De spirituali amicitia* that friendship is a step toward the love and the knowledge of God.[42]

Along the same lines, the Eastern Fathers—and, beginning with them, a tradition that leads to the Orthodox theology of the last two centuries—saw in friendship the highest expression of the mystical union between God and those created in his image. Pavel Florenskij dedicates part of his work *The Pillar and Foundation of Truth* (letter eleven) to friendship, and notes: "The mystical unity of two is a condition of knowledge and the manifestation of the spirit of truth who grants this knowledge."[43] Florenskij takes the teaching of Cicero and Aristotle, which Thomas also develops, to their furthest consequences. A friend is not only one who treats the friend as him or herself; friends constitute a bi-unity, a dyad. They are no longer merely what they were when taken individually, but something more: one soul. In this unity, each of the friends receives a confirmation of his or her own personality, finding his or her own "I" in the "I" of the other.[44]

---

[42] Aelred of Rievaulx, *De spirituali amicitia*, II, 18.
[43] Pavel Florenskij, *La colonna e il fondamento della verità* (Milan: Rusconi, 1974), 495.
[44] Cf. Ibid., 499.

Fraternal Friendships and Priesthood

The foregoing discussion of fraternity and friendship was intended, of course, to describe the essence of the Christian event, but it also had another goal: to point to an essential dimension of human experience itself. In other words, my intention was to describe both the fabric of being and of the being that entered into history, God-made-human, the fabric of the event that he inaugurated.

Now, what is true for every baptized person is true for every vocation rooted in Baptism—including the priesthood. Everything that is born from Baptism, in fact, participates in the particular structure that the sacrament gives to a person's life—the structure of communion—and, at the same time, expresses it. The experience of every Christian vocation, therefore, is necessarily fed by the experience of fraternity or friendship. There is no Christian vocation to a relationship with God that is not an event of communion; there is no experience of God without Christ, and no experience of Christ without the Church. For this reason, the word "fraternity," since it describes the essence of the Christian event, cannot be disconnected from the essence of priestly life; on the contrary, it takes on an historical and existential urgency for the times in which we are called to live. Today, no one can withstand the attacks stemming from this worldly mentality unless his or her affections are guided by a clear judgment of belonging. It is this judgment that not only makes possible, but also nourishes and makes attractive, the living out of virginity, poverty, and obedience that the priest (as every Christian, according to his or her state in life) is called to embrace. If I belong to my brother priests, I no longer belong to myself; my time, the things that I have, my money, my gifts, my relationships, are no longer my own.

Discovering this in one's own existence is something infinitely greater and more joyful than belonging to or keeping oneself. Keeping myself makes me small; discovering that I belong to other faces, who were called along with me, asserting to belong to the story of Christ in the world through those faces makes me great. The greatness of my person is given by the history of Christ among the people to whom I wish to belong in response to his call. I think that this point, which is both psychological and spiritual, captures the passage from nature to the new being to which Baptism calls each one of us.

But I want to develop these considerations even further. One can become an authentically Christian personality only by acknowledging the event of the fellowship into which Christ has inserted him or her and allowing him or herself to be generated by it. None of us can proceed toward the truth of our own being except through the change to which the presence of others impels us. The presence of the other changes our lives much more than the rains that over the ages furrow the earth and polish the rocks. Those who are placed at my side play the role of a sacrament.

In this sense, I would go so far as to say that, if we do not see our brother as an obstacle, we cannot love him. Unless we are altogether spiritualistic or superficial, we cannot help noticing, at certain moments of our life, the weight of the other who is placed at our side (for instance, in the workplace), the weight of his perceptions, background, and different personal temperament. These differences can show up even in someone whom we otherwise consider to be extraordinarily close. It is at this point that we discover the meaning of the sacramental presence of the other; we understand that his otherness or diversity is the sign of a Presence that transcends the other and makes him a sign of something more.

Gilbert Cesbron once said, "Every great existence is born of an encounter with a great chance."[45] In the fellowship of Christ, this great chance is offered to us in the other who is placed at our side. It is the greatness of the One who reaches me through the other placed at my side, and I note: not necessarily through the holiness of the other, but perhaps even through his poverty. The growth of the person is not a Herculean effort of the will; it is the fruit of the continual provocation of a true fellowship. "*Sufficentia nostra ex Deo*," says St. Paul (2 Cor 3:5). Others, when we desire, recognize, and welcome them as signs of his company, make us capable of becoming, in our turn, companions along the path of the people we meet.

Degenerations in Living out This Fellowship

As with all human things, the fellowship that is a sign of the mystery and the place of the presence of Christ can be lived in a reductive manner. When this happens, it means that our human criteria have prevailed over the novelty Christ has brought into human relationships. I want to outline schematically three forms of this degeneration.

A first possible degeneration is to see fellowship or friendship in Christ as a matter of duty. This would be a little like saying, "Since we are together, since Someone put us together, we have the duty of living our lives in common." The root of this degeneration is the misunderstand-

---

[45] G. Cesbron, *È mezzanotte dottor Schweitzer* (Milan: RCS Rizzoli Libri, 1993), 26.

ing of the true nature of charity, which is the event of the gratuity of Christ's love for us and of our response to this love. A moralistically reduced friendship is short-lived and almost always ends in violence. Christian fellowship, on the other hand, does not generate itself; it is not born mostly of the fruit of ascetic effort. It is first a gift, a grace; it lives on as a memory of this grace.

A second degenerate expression of fellowship in Christ is a community conceived and lived out as a kind of strategy: there is "strength in numbers," as we hear in an oft-cited proverb. Fellowship becomes a strategy in order to understand better, and to act more efficaciously (even in mission). This can be a subtle and dangerous temptation precisely because it plays upon sentiments of generosity and commitment that seem to be aspects of our love for Christ. The "illness" of this position lies once again in the fact that it bases everything on trust in ourselves and our own "doing".

A third and final degeneration is to conceive of friendship or fellowship as a sort of shelter, as a comfortable place, an escape from the world. The error here lies in considering the fellowship to be something nice, something that makes us happy, but in a naturalistic sense that distracts us from the mission that Christ entrusts to us in and with it. A fellowship understood in this sense becomes an agglomeration of solitudes, where in the end we seek in the other merely acquiescence to what we "feel" or "like." The meaning of a real Christian fraternal friendship is just the opposite: that God does not leave the one created in his image alone in the trial of existence. Solitude—that would be diabolical. Fellowship makes drama possible because it overcomes the tragedy of the person standing alone in the face of evil. This tragedy has been conquered, because Someone conquered it for us. Christ called the twelve not only to be with him, but "to send them" (Mk 3:14) to announce his victory.

IV
Far Apart in Order to Be Near

Staying as a Dimension of Leaving

Does passion for Christ consist in staying or in leaving? This is not an artificial question, since we are men and women whom Christ has called to live together forever, but the requirement of mission causes us to live far apart from one another.

The impetus that drives us out into the world to bring the gaze that has touched us is the same urgency that moved St. Paul: "For the love of Christ impels us, once we have come to the conviction that one died for all; therefore all have died. He indeed died for all, so that those who live might no longer live for themselves but for him who for their sake died and was raised" (2 Cor 5:14-15).

We live separated from one another as if we always lived together. The word "together" does not describe a socio-logical dimension, but describes that which constitutes the human being, that which allows a person to be him or herself. Community is not a group of persons who get together in order to accomplish something; communion is an essential dimension of the "I." Hence, there is a funda-mental priority of staying over leaving, an awareness that mission is not and cannot be the solitary and solipsistic song of a generous heart. Mission is the expansion of the communion that we live together.

In his recently published book, the German exegete Gerhard Lohfink comments on the verse in Mark's gospel, "He appointed twelve, whom he also named apostles, to be with him, and to be sent out" (Mk 3:14-15):

> The apostles' *being sent* implies their *being with* Jesus. This "being with" is not at all a provisionary remaining together which will soon be definitively resolved into mission. If this were the case, being with Jesus might too easily be understood as a limited and instrumental time, as a sort of retreat or introductory course. What really matters would come only afterwards: the time in which the twelve would be engaged like solitary combatants. We should not underestimate the force of this idea. In today's Church, it determines the way in which we view ecclesiastical authority and the apostolate much more deeply than we are perhaps aware. It's fine to be with Jesus—as one might describe this false image of apostolic reality—so long as one is sent out immediately afterwards. Of course, we get together every now and then to deepen our common faith, but then we leave again to live out our own missions in the world, on the scene, as individuals. But the plan of Mark's Gospel goes in a completely different direction.[46]

Mission therefore consists in expanding our fraternal friendships to those whom we meet, in the awareness that communion is given to us forever. One of my collabora-

---

[46] G. Lohfink, *Braucht Gott die Kirche?* (Freiburg: Herder, 1998), 219.

tors, Paolo Sottopietra, wrote to me regarding the above passage from Lohfink,

> The apostolic life is characterized by a being with Jesus that is permanent, definitive. This being with him is not a provisional, preparatory stage with respect to what is coming and would then constitute the true essence of this life. In other words, this shared life is not a preparatory phase for mission; it is a dimension of mission.... The essence of mission is to attract others to enter the intimacy of this shared life, this new kind of family.... Definitiveness is the trace of the action of God in human bonds; it is the sign of His initiative, creating and founding communion. The dimension of definitiveness cannot be produced by a merely human sharing of life. It points to another, present and operating factor, "the mystery of God which makes itself present among men... the nearness of Christ who dwells among us."[47]

In the years of formation, one is first of all called to comprehend or, better, to be comprehended by this being with Jesus. We can think of the paradox inherent in Jesus' command: "Remain in me" (cf. Jn 15:4-10). But he was going away! The next day he would be dead! Jesus repeats the word "remain" (ten times in seven verses!) to stress the definitive nature of the communion that had arisen between himself and his own. Remaining in him was to be

---

[47] P. Sottopietra, "Quando la missione ha sete di fraternità," in *Mondo e Missione* 8 (1998), 12.

the permanent and efficacious source of the apostles' missionary fruitfulness, they who very soon would be in Italy, Spain, and India, while one remained in Jerusalem.

The point of existence is to educate the heart and the mind to this communion as the form of life. It is impossible to live communion without sacrifice, without changing the self, without a conversion that takes place in infinitesimally small and constant corrections. Anyone who knows how to man a sailboat on high seas knows how important the tiniest of corrections can be when the winds and currents multiply effects to infinity. Life is like this too: a small correction can have infinite repercussions on our existence. For this reason, we must understand the reasons for our form of life and accept with flexibility the sacrifice that might be demanded of us. For example, we have to order our day to make the time allotted to us bear fruit, in the awareness of living entirely in the present. Doing this requires a constant conversion of heart. Sooner or later the moment will come in which the change required will seem difficult. It will look like the narrow door Jesus mentions in the Gospel (cf. Mt 7:13-14), but whoever does not have the courage to pass through this door cannot construct oneself.

This does not mean we have to cut things out of our life; rather, we are ensuring their eternity. If we want what has begun to mature fully, we must have the courage to follow a direction, to help our freedom to adhere to it. We must have a sense of the most important things, of the preciousness of our energies, of the task to which we are called. When a great athlete is preparing for a race—this is St. Paul's example (cf. 1 Cor 9:24-27)—nothing can become a distraction. If a great pianist wants to give a concert, he or she must practice hours and days and cannot be distracted by all the films hitting the box office, all the books being published, all the new things calling for attention. A passion for the common work must orient all our lives in this "remaining," and this involves effort. It is not a lack of activity but a construction of the self, from the synthesis that is born from the continuous comparison between one's self, one's desire, and that which is proposed.

The root of this "remaining" is charity. This charity becomes apparent in every instant, in every occasion which is given to us, in the enthusiasm of the relationships that are forged, in a passion for the understanding of life that study makes possible for us, and in a passion for the conscious plunging into the charism that has claimed us. Fellowship in destiny is fellowship in the present moment. So we understand, then, that mission is not something that happens tomorrow; mission is now. The field of mission is the whole world, but the world begins with the person. The beginning of mission is the transformation of the "I," and mission is the expansion of that changed "I" to embrace all the relationships, all the persons, all the circumstances and events that will be given to it to live. "One is not sent at the beginning, once and for all," notes Sottopietra; "one *is* (permanently) sent."[48] The world's new dawn depends on the truth with which we enter into this "remaining," beginning in the years of formation, not as something that we first learn and then later apply, but as a new dimension of life that has no end.

---

[48] Ibid.

Christ Willed Us to Be Together

For those who acknowledge Christ, there are infinite degrees of "being together." The most basic is that which is required of everyone in the Church: the Sunday Eucharistic celebration. The degree requested of those of us in the Fraternity of St. Charles is more intense: to be together all the day long. For this reason, if our being together is not the place of a permanent initiative of our "I," it will inevitably degrade into a mere juxtaposition of existences.

God allows amazing things to happen when he calls people to live together around someone whom he has called, so that the extraordinary finality Christ brings to human life might shine through a particular person. I want to give two examples to illustrate the power of such events. While we were struck by the outpouring of grief at the death of Enzo Piccinini, we were even more struck by the witness of his life.[49] Enzo had a naturally "total" personality. Perhaps this is why Christ chose him, as he chose St. Paul; they were personalities who lived "totally" and thus became factors of an exemplary, meaningful and moving constructivity. Another example can be taken from the study I am currently engaged in on the origins of the movement Communion and Liberation. I was impressed by the fact that the movement was born in so many cities because Fr. Giussani sent people there who were close to him. When closeness is a constant movement of one person towards the other, what happens can be so powerful!

---

[49] A highly esteemed surgeon and the leader of the Communion and Liberation movement in Bologna, Italy, who died in an automobile accident on May 26, 1999.

The risk is always present of avoiding the urgent necessity of building up the person; each person must be brought, with all his or her gifts, exaltations, limitation and sins, to the measure of the role of protagonist willed by Christ. This role as protagonist is not the production of a sort of Nietzchean "overman". Rather, it consists in a responsibility: a response of gratitude in the present, a response to an Other who is making us. The years of formation are decisive ones. The seed which has been scattered in them will flower; the seed which has not been scattered will have great difficulty coming to fruition. Later grafts often yield precarious results and can even compromise the balance of life in the ecosystem. More clearly, I would say that there is the risk that our enthusiasm is not strong enough. Without a permanent sense of wonder, there cannot be mission.

All that happens in our world, in the Church, or to each one of us, is a factor of our life. It intersects our existence and should become more and more a theme of conversation, reflection, and work. When conversations are banal, it is a sign that the heart is more sensitive to the sentimental reflection of what strikes it than to the objectivity of what is happening, through which God wishes to rouse the earth and its inhabitants. Christ places the person within a real, human, solicited, and guided fellowship. If each of us cannot see this every morning as a miraculous work of God, or of mercy, everything will be spoiled by our touch. What has not been taken up is not saved, as the Fathers said. This is not only true at the beginning, the Incarnation (the Word becoming man); it is decided moment by moment.

It is a miraculously revolutionary fact that Christ willed us to be together. To my mind, nothing so resembles creation out of nothing. If Christ placed others together with me, it is not merely because this is meaningful only for us; it is meaningful for all. What God works is always for all.

What Makes Us Protagonists in Human History

My chief desire is constantly to reawaken wonder in the face of the fact that we have been placed together. What I mean is above all ontological: we in the Fraternity of St. Charles have been placed together around an event, around the fact that—whether it is recognized or not— Christ chose Fr. Giussani as he has chosen other men and women, to give a different countenance to humanity in our time.

We are very aware that there is only one thing that brings human beings to their truth and happiness: he who created and redeemed them. Our wonder is born of the fact that Christ has placed us together so that we might be, through the experience of unity that we live, the sacrament of the newness that he wants to bring, first of all among us. If this does not happen among us, it cannot happen outside of us. Mission is possible only as the echo of a lived fraternal friendship, because it is the echo of a forgiveness that has been received. My brothers and sisters are the sacrament of the forgiveness of Christ, of his incarnate love for my life.

Familiarity with the Church's history helps us to discern the newness that the Spirit is always bringing forth in it. It nourishes our gratitude for this newness, which only then can be such for all others. A passage from Van der Meer's book, *Augustine the Bishop; the Life and Work of a Father of the Church*, which describes the complexity of the Church's life in fourth century Africa, helps us to understand the situation of the people of that time and to see that we are placed within an uninterrupted flow of history.

As soon as he [Augustine] was elevated to the episcopacy and became the leader of a group of clerics, he discreetly tried to bring about a reform. He proposed to his clerics the adoption of a form of common life, which he himself had led up to that point with several companions animated by the same ideas (first as a community of philosophers at Cassiciaco, then, following their return to Africa, as a group of lay monks, then as a group of priests at Tagaste and later at Hippo, and finally, after his episcopal ordination, with his priests). His episcopal residence was transformed into a monastery or, in other words, into a community of priests, deacons, and sub-deacons. All of these lived under the direction of the bishop, though there were no novices or lay brothers, and all observed the same rule. Monastic life and pastoral activity had remained very separate things in the West, until Eusebius of Vercelli began to unify them upon his return from Egypt (around 340), living in community with the clerics of his cathedral. Eusebius thus became, according to the testimony of St. Ambrose, the first initiator of the *vita communis*. His example was quickly followed by Paulinus of Nola, by Victor, the former soldier who became the bishop of Rouen, by Augustine between 391 and 396, and shortly thereafter, by another famous ex-soldier, Martin of Tours. It is not clear that Augustine was aware of these other attempts to form a common life. The plan he inaugurated at Hippo unmistakably bears the mark of his genius and corresponds to old projects which he had not yet been able to realize. In any case, it was he who first introduced the clerical common life to Africa. It was obviously impossible for him to lead in his episcopal residence the sort of retired life that had once been his, in the monastery adjacent to the cathedral; a bishop who did not receive visits would be inhuman. So he sought another solution. His house remained open to everyone, but the private residences of priests who lived isolated from one another disappeared. What Augustine had twice tried to do with companions who shared his ideals, he did now, no longer with companions he had chosen, but with his collaborators in the sacred ministry. The common life was a very practical ideal: it gave those who participated in it the possibility of mutually perfecting one another. It was a testing place of ideas, an open circle, the dream of great spirits whose goal is the communication of this life.[50]

We find another important passage in a page of Thomas of Celano's life of St. Francis of Assisi:

When there were eight disciples, blessed Francis gathered them together, and, after having spoken to them at length of the Kingdom of God, of despising the world, of denying one's own will, and of the mastery one must exert over one's own body, he divided them into four pairs and said to them, "Go, beloved,

---

[50] F. Van der Meer, *Sant'Agostino pastore d'anime*, (Cinisello Balsamo, Milan: Edizioni Paoline, 1971), 459-462.

two by two to all the various places of the world and proclaim peace and penitence in the remission of sins. Be patient in persecutions, certain that the Lord will accomplish his will and keep his promises. Respond humbly to those who interrogate you, bless those who persecute you, and thank those who curse and insult you, because the everlasting Kingdom is being prepared for us in exchange." And the disciples, receiving this precept of holy obedience with great joy and gladness, prostrated themselves before the blessed father, who embraced them with tenderness and devotion and said to each one, "Place your trust in the Lord, and he will care for you." This was the phrase he repeated each time he sent a brother to carry out obedience. Thus brother Bernard and brother Egidio left for the sanctuary of St. James in Compostela, in Galicia; St. Francis took another companion and chose the valley of Rieti; and the remaining four, two by two, headed out in the other two directions. But after a short while, St. Francis, wishing to see them all again, prayed to the Lord who gathered the scattered children of Israel, that he might deign to reunite them soon. And immediately, according to his desire, they found themselves together without any of them having been called back, and they gave thanks to God. Taking food together, they showed the warmth of their joy in seeing their pious shepherd once again, and their wonder that they had all had the same thought [of returning]. They recounted the graces they had received from the merciful Lord and they requested and humbly obtained correction and penance from the blessed father for their faults of negligence or ingratitude. This is what they always did when they returned to him; they did not hide from him the smallest of thoughts and involuntary motions of the soul, and after they had accomplished everything that had been commanded of them, they esteemed themselves worthless servants. Truly, "purity of heart" filled this first group of disciples of the blessed Francis to such a point that, although they were aware of accomplishing useless, holy, and righteous things, they were utterly incapable of drawing vainglory from their work. Then the blessed Francis, drawing his sons to himself with great love, began to reveal to them his proposals, and those things which the Lord had revealed to him."[51]

We in the Communion and Liberation movement have been called to carry the exciting form of life begun by Fr. Giussani into the world. But within that great people which is the movement, we in the Fraternity have a particular vocation. In comparison with fathers of families, we undoubtedly have an easier day. Twenty-four hours a day we are helped to live out that to which all everyone is called, but we are not awakened at three in the morning by a crying baby who insists on being fed and burped. Our life is easier in this respect, and so our responsibility is greater: Christ has called us and has given us this simplified life so that we can help others. Those who have families to care for are in the front lines; we are the rear guard, like those who have to run back and forth bringing the soldiers munitions and food. But we are not the rear guard that runs away!

---

[51] *Fonti francescane*, (Assisi: Movimento francescano, 1978), 434-435.

In a certain sense, the heart of what I want to say is more or less ineffable: it is the surprise for the sake of which God made us. Up until fifteen years ago, I had never dreamed of the idea of a priestly fraternity, nor had I imagined myself in charge of priests and seminarians. God does what he wills. I am convinced that most of us would have been good fathers of families, but this is not how God reasons. He chooses in order to do what is interesting to *him*. Evidently, he is interested in carrying something out through us, and we will discover what it is. We have understood that the one thing that very clearly interests him is that we are to live the unity among ourselves not as the result of rules or commands, and not as the fruit of canonical institutions, but as the most precious event of our lives. To live truly, with truth, implies a resurrection, a continual beginning again, since our perception of what God is doing is constantly failing because of forgetfulness, distraction, heaviness of heart, or hardness of head.

The first goal of the Fraternity is to open our eyes to the activity of God. What he allows me to understand right now is that, within the Fraternity, the perception of communion is still very vague; our memory, our conversation, the way in which we treat one another, the initiatives of individual members toward others are still too little determined by it. So do we have to change our conversation or the way we treat one another? This would be a dead end. What must change is our memory of what God makes happen.

The great drama of our time is that we live within a society that wants to make our awareness foggy. Consequently, life becomes mediocre. But one does not extract oneself from mediocrity with a project; one escapes it with a question posed to Christ and to the other.

I mentioned the movement of the "I". By this expression I mean the refusal to accept living a single instant, to a greater or lesser extent, without the presence of Christ within that instant. Even the tiniest instant, like when I meet someone on the street or in a hallway of the house, demands this movement of the "I," so that there is no instant which is superfluous or without meaning. This is exactly the opposite of what the world lives. The world wants to forget, to be distracted, to have no memory; it is afraid of this movement because it has not known Christ.

What made St. Paul, St. Augustine, St. Francis protagonists in human history, what made Fr. Giussani such a protagonist, is the fact that Christ left such a burning mark upon their lives that the meaninglessness of the instant is no longer possible. This is a particular grace that God gives to some (and he calls them by name); we, on the other hand, are allowed to participate in it, to desire it. The years of priestly formation are the occasion for this new root, this new perception of the self to mature, so that with time it will grow and bear fruit anywhere. This is not a perception that one can learn by reading a book; it must be communicated, as Plato says, from flame to flame, *lumen de lumine*.[52]

---

[52] Cf. Plato, *Letter* VII, 341D: "There neither is nor will be a treatise of mine on the subject. For it does not admit of exposition like branches of knowledge; but after much converse about the matter itself and a life lived together, suddenly a light, as it were, is kindled in the soul by a flame that leaps to it from another, and thereafter sustains itself."

V
The Path to Christ[53]

"I Am Here for You"

How real is the presence of Christ, the person of Christ for me? "You shall not take the name of the Lord your God in vain," says the first of the commandments (Ex 20:7). We can, however, confess his name with our lips without it corresponding to a real person. On the other hand, everything is in a certain sense complicated by the fact that he is present but invisible, or, at least, his visibility does not have the same proportions as the things and persons we encounter every day. But all of this has to have a meaning! His invisibility must facilitate his visibility, otherwise his own word would be meaningless: "It is to your advantage that I go away" (Jn 16:7).

The greatest risk we can run in life is that of living our love for Christ without perceiving him as an ever-present Thou. We can live virginity as a sort of unrequited love, according to the famous expression, "They claim to love God because they don't love anyone." Our personal and communal path must meet and overcome this risk. This is a question that will remain open until the final encounter, when the face of God will be revealed. But keeping the

---

[53] The following reflections were inspired by a dinner conversation between Fr. Giussani and a group of *Memores Domini*, now published in L. Giussani, *L'attrattiva Gesù* (Milan: BUR, 1999), 147-160.

question open is not enough; it must prompt a real dialogue between ourselves and him.

When I first met Fr. Giussani, I was very struck by his insistence on community as the visibility of Christ. I understood that this insistence was not something secondary; it urged us to think about the historical presence of Christ—Christ as a present event, not as something far removed from me—and went against the grain of the individualism, pietism, and sentimentalism so present in the Catholicism of the 1950s. Pietism involves limiting one's relationship with Christ to an act of emotion, a devotional manifestation, to something which resolves itself into certain expressions of piety, but which does not touch one's daily existence. The Christian people is the flowering of the event of Christ. The people that we are, or that we are called to generate, is the flowering of this familiarity with Christ. Without this relationship to the "Thou" of Christ, the flower withers; little by little, it dries out until nothing remains but the exterior form.[54] What I am saying does not mean that we forget the sacramental presence of Christ in his body. Rather, we must go to the personal root of this sacramental reality.

If I had to sum up my guiding pedagogical preoccupation in a single word, I would choose the word "sign". This is what I want to help myself and those around me to see: the event of Christ does not remain something exterior, but enters into a person's life and carries it to fulfillment. This happens, however, only if the person adheres to a human place, which is the sign of Jesus in the present moment.

---

[54] Lit. "addressing Christ as 'Thou'" (Italian Tu), the familiar form of address reserved for family and close friends [—Tr.].

Christ reaches us through the carnality of persons and circumstances behind which he remains veiled. Why does he do this? So that he can be contemporary to each person. His individual, singular, and unmistakable personality remains veiled behind the sign in order to be present, here and now, to all. Through signs and circumstances, however, he asks for and offers a personal relationship with each person. This is a paradox of visibility and hiddenness: he is present, seen and unseen. We touch him and do not touch him. Friendship is a sacramental sign of Christ, but at the same time it does not exhaust his person; it points to him, because without this reference, the sign would sooner or later degenerate into a possession and be darkened or extinguished.

If someone were to ask me now why I am in the Fraternity of St. Charles, why I find myself together with certain persons, the only true and complete response would be, "I am here for you, O Christ." "I am here for you": this response names Christ as the relationship at the source of a life's decisions. It means: I am here because I have recognized Christ's love for me, and, in the words of St. John, I know that "he first loved us" (1 Jn 4:19). It is difficult to understand and to experience what it means to love Christ, but it is easier to understand that Christ has loved and loves us. These are facts: he has allowed us to know him (faith), to meet him (vocation), and has created a place in which he daily receives us. Thus the sign flowers in a continual reference to his person, unseen and yet seen, as "in a mirror, dimly" (1 Cor 13:12). "I am here for you" refers not only to the cause, his love for us, but also to the response, the meaning of every instant.

The reason why Christ placed us together is expressed in St. Pius X's catechism: "To know him, love him, and serve him in this life, and to enjoy him in the next."[55] The Gospel says the same: "That they should know you and the one whom you sent" (Jn 17:3). So the point of our fellowship is knowing him together. It is like a competition among friends who are together in order to tell each other, moment by moment, what they discover about Christ. Isn't the history of the Church the story of a progressive discovery of Christ? What would be the point of loving the Church and her history if this were not a discovery of the person of Christ? The Church's history is the person of Christ expanded in time, and the study of this history is the knowledge of the person of Christ expanded in time.

Sometimes people and things seem more concrete to me than Christ; they are right in front of me, I hold them in my hands! This is precisely the challenge of faith: through the things we can touch and the people facing us, we can slowly discern the face taking shape in these things, the face of the One revealing himself through them. The reason for silence and prayer is that "our gaze seeks a face in the night."[56] Silence makes it possible for us to perceive the transparency of things. This is why I am always struck by St. Peter's affirmation, "Although you have not see him, you love him" (1 Pt 1:8). It is not true that we have seen nothing, or we would not be able to love him, but we have not yet seen the fulfillment of the sign. Our being here for him together and our desire and demand to know him anticipate the fulfillment of his self-manifestation, according to the last word of the Bible: "*Maranathà!*" (Rev 22: 20). Come, show yourself!

---

[55] Cf. "Catechismo della dottrina cristiana pubblicato per ordine del Sommo Pontefice san Pio X," in *Il Sabato* (Milan 1992), 16.

[56] From the hymn "Prima che sorga l'alba" (from the Trappist monastery at Vitorchiano), in *Canti*, 150.

In order for a person to believe in Christ, he must first know him, and in order to know him in his concrete, historical personality, he must in a certain sense spend time with him, just as the apostles and first disciples spent time with him and drew their faith in him from this direct experience. It still holds true today that in order to believe in Christ, a person must in some manner and measure repeat the experience of the first disciples. Like them, he must hear Jesus speaking, see him acting, working miracles, weeping, suffering, dying, rising, and ascending into heaven. In this way, the believer will penetrate, little by little, into the soul of this man called Jesus; he will enter into his thoughts and emotions.[57]

Love's Itinerary

In the refrain of one of the songs of a Dominican songwriter, Fr. Cocagnac, we find, "*Si Dieu ne nous aimait pas il n'aurait pas fait la terre... il n'aurait pas fait tout ça*" ("If God hadn't loved us, he wouldn't have made the world... he wouldn't have done all that").[58] The discovery of the world becomes the discovery of the love which brought it into being. We move from things to their origin, and discover, at this origin, a personal love: "If God hadn't loved us," if God hadn't loved us with a personal love.

---

[57] G. Corti, "Alla radice della controversia kerigmatica," in *La Scuola Cattolica*, IV-V (1950), 301.

[58] A. M. Cocagnac, "Si Dieu ne nous aimait pas," in *Canti biblici*, supplement to the periodical *Tracce: Litterae Communionis*, a. XXVI, n. 1 (January 1999), 12.

How can I respond to such a love? How do I connect with it? How do I live in the face of it? How do I let it permeate my days? Most basically, how do I fall in love with Christ?

What does it mean, to fall in love with Christ? This is a fundamental question in the path to him. Whereas in most cases, human love arises as an emotion that then puts down roots in an act of judgment, love for Christ is born of a judgment which then "expands" into an emotion. In this path that runs from judgment to affection, we must ask, "Who are you, unknown Savior?" so that our lives are slowly transformed in the experience of knowing him. We ask so that we can recognize the One whom John the Baptist describes: "Among you stands one whom you do not know" (Jn 1:26). We ask to know him always anew, so that we may never take his newness for granted. We ask it so that we might be granted a continuity of life; so that in every instant we might live in the attitude of the beggar.

Our love for Christ "is a judgment of the intellect that draws all our sensibility, all of human emotion, with it... Love—and not only 'love for Christ'—is and implies a judgment. A judgment is a recognition of truth; it is a recognition of being."[59] A judgment—so logic tells us—is the relationship between a subject and a predicate; hence, it implies recognition on the part of the subject, a gaze that recognizes the evidence of being and marvels at it. We see, then, that there is a circular relationship between judgment and affection. Love arises because of the recognition of the truth of a thing, as a gaze full of wonder in the face

---

[59] L. Giussani, "Natale: motivo della vita come lavoro," insert in *Tracce: Litterae Communionis*, a. XXV, n. 11 (December 1998), VI.

of reality. Such a gaze gives rise to the evidence that guides a life. The path of love begins as a judgment and draws affection after it, but even at the beginning it implies affection as a factor; it implies a wonder that makes the lover adhere to the being he or she has recognized as a mysterious presence that makes itself felt. So it is grace that makes him or her recognize the other's presence and the presence of an Other behind it.

Wonder gives rise to the judgment of the intellect. Why does the reality I encounter (a friend, a loved one, a book, a sunset) respond to something that I am? Why does a jumble of musical notes on a page, once played, awaken a feeling of correspondence in me? The understanding born of wonder formulates a judgment: it moves from a recognition that the reality involved is created to the discovery of God's intervention and becoming man. This is the understanding of faith (*intellectus fidei*), the capacity God gives to the human being so that he or she might trace the whole itinerary from the creatureliness of things to their Creator and Savior. This judgment, however, can only exist with our help. We must work to keep it alive lest we begin to take the newness we have encountered for granted and allow ourselves to be conquered by aridity. Work is the instant lived in the awareness of eternity; it is the link between the present moment and the eternal. Hence it is a demand made of Christ, that he show himself in the words that I speak, in the page I am studying, in the darkness that makes everything seem like an enemy to me, in the sadness that threatens to overpower me. Every one of our demands is always a response to something that has preceded us.

The first step towards loving Christ is remembering that he has loved us, that he loves us! To love Christ is to respond to something that has already begun: the history of his predilection for us. If our life is a river, Christ has carved out the riverbed, and we have only to follow it. In Paul Claudel's play, *The Tidings Brought to Mary*, we are reminded that love is not kissing the leper; it is remaining in one's place with an awareness of the Infinite.[60] Without this, love would become an abstract and impossible sentiment, because it would lack a point of reference.

How do I fall in love with Christ? I must respond to his love, which has already expressed itself. I do not know if this love will transform itself into the fire of a St. Teresa of Avila or the last months of "atheism" suffered by St. Thérèse of Lisieux, or if it will mean the total hiddenness of the cloister or the activity of Gregory Barbarigo, the bishop of Bergamo, who chose as his motto, "My ministry is doing." Everything changes not when sudden flames of emotion are sparked in us, but when our dedication becomes a response to a gratuitousness that has preceded us. The concrete signs of his predilection make up our personal history. For this reason, to pray is always to remember; it is the conscious memory of a predilection that has gone before us.

Familiarity with Christ as a Factor of History

On many occasions, I have asked myself what might be the root of that peculiar characteristic of the Christian soul: joy. This word, "joy," indicates the echo in the present

---

[60] Cf. P. Claudel, *The Tidings Brought to Mary*, trans. Wallace Fowlie (Chicago: Gateway, 1960), 15.

moment of that to which we are destined. Joy is the fore-taste, in the present, of the port toward which we yearn. It is an anticipation of the end, which fills the hours of the journey with its light, making them more conscious, free, and easy. Joy is born of the judgment that we are on the right path, and of the perception of an Other in whom we find all our strength. This is what allows us to journey unhindered through days and trials. The absence of joy means that the person has been uprooted, whether through a lack of awareness (the loss of memory) or through disorientation (the loss of self in things, in anxieties, or in responsibilities).

There is a link between joy and the experience of one's own usefulness: we are happy when we know that we are being useful, and this usefulness comes about when we serve others, beginning with those whom Christ has called together with us. If joy is certitude that the final plenitude is already present here and now, the sense of "usefulness" is the desire that this plenitude transform life. So what is useful? What does the usefulness of life consist in? Or, better, how can I be of use for the truth of the world and the good of human beings? "It is not for the stone to choose its place," we read in *The Tidings Brought to Mary*.[61] Usefulness is recognizing the place that the Master Artisan assigns to our life; it is following him, following his indications, and entering into his sign. The greatest usefulness of our lives lies in entering the place Christ has created, so that this might be of use to the world. He died "for us and for our salvation". This is why obedience is joy; it is the sure and transcendent cause of joy.

---

[61] Ibid., 14.

Life changes when we work together, because working together is radically different from working alone. Working together is a sacramental fact, as Jesus said: "For where two or three are gathered together in my name, I am there among them" (Mt 18:20). It is possible to work together even when we are alone, but this is more difficult. Working together, studying together, praying together, makes it easier to recognize the sacrament that is being realized through this gesture. For this reason, working together is communion made concrete, making present the mysterious sacrament of his presence. It changes the way we look at problems, the way we approach things, because the guiding principle is no longer my or someone else's intelligence, but a sacramental factor: Christ's authority.

We understand, then, that familiarity with Christ involves our whole life, as both a personal and historical dimension. This familiarity is possible only within a people. It is the desire to discover the root of our belonging, to journey along the path together, asking to go all the way to the end; it means discerning the secret origin of every step of the people we are a part of; it is "acknowledging Christ as the most important factor of my life."[62] Thus there is a profound connection between living a permanent dialogue with Christ and desiring that the people to whom we belong might continually be regenerated and grow in awareness, in passion, and in the ability to communicate themselves.

If we do not rejoice at the grace God has given to our lives in allowing us to be part of this people, there can be

---

[62] L. Giussani, *Generare trace nella storia del mondo*, (Milan: Rizzoli, 1998), 131-132.

no familiarity with Christ. In the same way, there can be no passion for the history of a people if there is no silence at the heart of our days. But the ability to remain in the presence of the Mystery is not something that can be acquired all at once; it is the fruit of a long and continual demand:

> Prayer must fast before it feasts; it must be nakedness of heart before it is the heavenly mantel upon which the worlds dance.... Perhaps a day will come in which God will allow you to enter brutally, as an axe enters the flesh of the tree, and to fall madly, like a stone, into the night of waters, and to flow singing, like fire, into the heart of metal. And on that day, you will know of what flesh the world is made, and you will speak freely to the soul of the world of the Tree, the Water, and Metal.... All this may one day happen, my dear child, when the serpent has shed its skin. But one must begin at the beginning: this is essential.[63]

"Teach Me Jesus Christ, for I Wish to Find Him"

> "Teach me Jesus Christ, for I wish to find him;
> I have been told he is enamored of me.
> I pray you, teach me my love...."[64]

This citation from Jacopone of Todi's *Lauds* reveals the attitude with which we should respond to the call of Christ.

---

[63] O. V. Milosz, *Miguel Mañara*, (Milan: Jaca Book, 1998), 50-51.

[64] Jacopone da Todi, *Le laudi* (Florence: Libreria Editrice Fiorentina, 1955), 129.

He has placed us together so that we can find him more deeply than we could have imagined. Christ loves us; this is not an idea or an emotion, but a proclamation that reaches the person. Our life is given to us so that we can recognize this reality.

If, in the years of formation, this love for Jesus does not take root, if it does not completely inform the relationships we have with one another, a real, indestructible tie cannot be formed between us that will be capable of surviving the pressures of the world, time, and distance. But the more Jesus is at the center of our lives, the stronger these ties become, and the more clearly the sign begins to take on the features of the Word made flesh. This is the condition of our being together in truth, the path along which we respond to the voice calling us to life, calling us every instant to live and to give our lives away. This path can be taken up only with a wisdom greater than our own, with a power of forgiveness that surpasses our measure.

Christ remains only a word, at most the end point of an emotion or discussion, if he is not first recognized as a person who is present, who is always taking the initiative in our regard, and who for that reason awaits our response. He has placed us side by side with people precisely so that we might notice his initiative and respond to him. So we see clearly now how necessary others are for our happiness. This is a fundamental truth of our existence.

A relationship with Christ always begins with his initiative; hence, the beginning of the relationship is adoration, or wonder. There can be no adoration without wonder, and there can be no wonder that does not become adoration. This is true of the love between a man and a woman, of a father for his child, or of a friend for a friend.

A relationship with Christ goes beyond momentary emotions or moods. In a second step, the relationship does indeed fill both emotions and moods, but at the beginning, it is a recognition that he has taken the initiative and always takes it, at every moment: "he has first loved us" (1 Jn 4:19). This is a concrete reality whose depths we will never exhaust; only certain experiences of the love of a mother or certain moments of truth in a friendship can give us a glimpse of something of the tireless love of Christ. He takes the initiative in my regard, through the faces he has placed at my side; thus, when I acknowledge that the faces of these friends are more important than my mood at the moment, I am looking at myself with truth.

Christ's love is a personal love. He loves us personally and completely, even when we do evil, even when we forget him. Even in our collapse, in our sin, or in the most extreme weakness, there is always the possibility of getting up again. This possibility flows from Jesus' love, or, better yet, from the memory of his personal love for me. St. Paul says, "The life I now live in the flesh I live by faith in the Son of God, who loved me and gave himself for me" (Gal 2:20). It is in this key, terrible but glorious, that the cross must dominate our lives, first as the astonished contemplation of how far Christ went for each one of us. Then, in consequence, this contemplation becomes an entering into what is contemplated. It becomes a gift of oneself in love for him that, precisely because it is done freely and in love, no longer measures. It can no longer measure either the sensibility of the gift or its results.

There are three ways in which we express our awareness of Christ's love for us and ask that our love for him grow.

The first is the word: a person who does not speak to his beloved does not love him. Our day is full of occasions of speech: there are the psalms, the Mass or the liturgy, the time of silence. There is, however, an infinite distance between speaking *of* Christ and speaking *to* him. All the words we speak to Christ must be the expressions of our heart and understanding; they must constantly be redeemed from the routine that turns every word of love into a ritual, a thing to fill up the intolerable silence.

The second way is that of the imagination: the lives of the apostles allow us to understand the present by shaping it in the light of their experience with Jesus, awakening our desire to "copy" his humanity.

The third way is adoration: only in the awareness of the infinite superiority of God can we be familiar with him. Adoration is the acknowledgement that he is greater than any human measure, wiser than our greatest wisdom, truer than our greatest truth, more beautiful than our greatest beauty, holier than our greatest holiness. Before his face, we remain disciples, always children.

The love of Christ precedes everything about me. How difficult it is, though, for us to convince ourselves of this when life takes a different turn from the one we imagined, when a friendship is broken or a loved one is lost! We see then that if we are not in dialogue with him, if we do not desire to "copy" his humanity, if we do not give ourselves to him, his "precedence" takes us by surprise. Sometimes it even scandalizes or painfully wounds us.

In order to learn love for Christ, affection for him, I point to two privileged means: song and works of charity. Singing is the supreme form of our speaking familiarly with Christ; if we keep this in mind, we would sing the psalms differently. At the same time, songs are ways of expressing a humanity we have learned, a humanity we must ask for. This humanity is infinitely nuanced; we catch a fragment, a glimmer, a ray of it in the Renaissance hymns of Tommaso da Victoria, in Beethoven, in a Negro spiritual, or even in a song by Claudio Chieffo.[65]

Works of charity, time freely given so that we might share in other people's lives, are an identification with the form of Christ's humanity. This form is gratuitousness: he came in order to share our life and death so that we might share in his divinity, through the infinite depth of his humanity.

In the path to Christ, the word "sacrifice" is important. The more one loves, the more one "needs sacrifice" on which to base the thing that one loves, so that "what comes 'first' in the relationship will show itself"; thus the relationship "becomes ever truer and no longer risks disappearing—that is to say, it becomes eternal."[66] The desire inside of us can be compared to a pilot's need to orient him or herself by the stars, except that the compass guiding our ship is confused by a thousand magnets, throwing us off course. The truth of our path can only be affirmed if we continually affirm its original direction. This is sacrifice: a human verification, the correction needed for our desire to be realized according to its truth, a repair made en route so that the ship can reach its port. Sacrifice is something positive, the passage to a greater, truer, and more deeply affirmed reality. Of course, it too participates in that inexplicable mystery in which there can be no good in life without evil, whether this evil be moral, physical, or even metaphysical. "These two cities are indistinguish-

---

[65] A contemporary Italian Catholic songwriter. [— Tr.]

[66] L. Giussani, *L'attrativa Gesù*, 29.

able," writes Augustine[67]: the city of God and the city of men and women, good and evil, are inextricably joined. We have been freed so that we could be free. Here lies the reason behind the attractiveness of sacrifice.

The Imagination and Present Experience

Our path to Christ does not begin from nothing, i. e., the isolated "I" does not construct something out of nothing through imagination. What we imagine of Christ must be anchored in the objectivity of a present experience, the experience of himself which Christ gives to us within the reality of our lives. Imagination means allowing this experience to flower as a permanent question and as a dialogue with him who is among us.

This imagination cannot be some kind of abstract "mysticism." It is identification, placing oneself in the story, and not a sentimental game; it arises from the desire to risk the elements of a present experience. We remember the astonished words spoken by a young girl to one of our priests during an outing near Novosibirsk (Siberia): "The same thing that happened to them has happened to us!" The "they" she refers to are the apostles. She had gone to the outing to see what had happened to them, to John and Andrew (cf. Jn 1:35-39), and discovered, to her surprise, elements of her own experience. This seems to me to be something fundamental; when we fail to stress it, the imagination remains an ado-

---

[67] Cf. St. Augustine, De civitate Dei I, 35L "Perplexae quippe sunt istae duae civitates in hoc saeculo invicemque permixtae, donec ultimo iudicio dirimantur" ("The two cities are in fact indistinguishable in the flow of time; they are intermixed, until the last judgment effects their separation").

lescent phenomenon which can become a refuge, distancing us from reality rather than immersing us in it. Identification, on the other hand, does not remove us from the present, but points us to it with an infinitely greater richness, power of intelligence, adhesion, humor, and ability to get up again. Most of all, it gives us a passion for the glory of Christ.

Christianity is an experience that begins now, but it is nurtured by an ability to identify with the past, with the humanity of Christ described in the Gospels, with the apostles' experience of Christ. This is why we take John and Andrew's encounter with Jesus, described in chapter one of the Gospel of John (Jn 1:35-39), as paradigmatic.

I am in a community. There has been a call. I want to deepen this experience so that it does not lose its truth. Our present, given to us by Christ, is not only the inescapable starting point for our demand for his face; every present experience also contains a prophecy which brings us back to the origins. It is always the prophecy of the Church that connects our present experience to the origins.

In Fr. Giussani, we find an example of identification with the origin which has come about by applying a phrase from the Old Testament to Jesus:

> "If thy presence will not go with me, do not carry us up from here" (Ex 33:15). If you take these words, which Moses speaks to God, and address them to Jesus, think: how true they are! There is absolutely no artificiality in them, and they are not out of place. What density and specificity of meaning they have! How they obligate you to the right and the true!"[68]

---

[68] L. Giussani, *L'attrativa Gesù*, 189-190.

It is easy to think of examples: we can say the psalms every day for years, at morning and evening prayer, without them becoming a personal word. We can listen to the Scriptures being read aloud every day at Eucharistc Celebration, without the slightest tremor awakening in us.

The scope of the imagination is to make us identify with Jesus' humanity. Through this, we learn from him how to see, how to think, how to relate to people. His humanity gave birth to the tradition of the Church, the representation of this humanity throughout the precariousness of time, where the gold shines through the clay and mud. Every form of art has this great, divine capacity. Again, Fr. Giussani teaches us:

> How important art is, from this point of view! How it supports our efforts! Think of how many images of Jesus we find in art, many of them so moving! When, in my first year of high school, I placed on my desk an image of Carracci's Jesus, which you have heard me mention so many times, I was sure, critical of myself but sure, that it was no great masterpiece. And yet it reminded me of the presence of a countenance that was greater, more beautiful, and more powerful.[69]

Every real act of imagination is prayer. In order to enter into and identify with the book of the gospel, one must first ask Christ, invoke him. How can we be assured that our imagination is not a projection onto the past of something

---

[69] *Ibid.,* 192-193.

that was not really there? It is the origin itself which must be invited to reveal itself. An imaginative involvement in the events of Christ's life is an expression of our love for him, of the maturity of the tie of affection that binds us to his person. It is our esteem for him that is capable of refining our sensibility, pointing it toward the secret of that enormous humanity. But this secret is his total relativity to the Father. This is not something we can possess through our understanding, as if it were some great but well-defined thing. For this reason, there is no authentic tension towards identification with Christ's humanity if we do not ask to live the relationship which constitutes it: Christ's relationship to the Father.

VI
Urgent Issues for Priestly Formation in Our Time

The Real Man

Anyone reading the texts published by the Roman Congregations, from the time of Vatican Council II until today, regarding the formation of priests or of young men called to the priesthood will be struck by how much space they dedicate to the candidate's "human formation." This is true particularly of texts from the Congregation for Catholic Education and the Congregation for the Clergy. This stress points to a serious need that must be taken into consideration. I refer to the need for young men preparing for the priesthood—who will be the future leaders of the community and the form of its existence—to be people who have taken this path, not for fear of other possibilities or primarily out of renunciation, but because they have seen an authentic possibility for the realization of their own humanity.[70]

---

[70] Actually, the conciliar decree on priestly formation, *Optatam Totius*, did not dedicate a separate chapter to human formation, as is the case in later documents. However, in the fourth chapter (nos. 4-7), while discussing the need for greater attention to be paid to spiritual formation, the text spoke of human maturity (no. 11), which was identified above all in a firm spirit and in a capacity to make decisions and judge both persons and events in a balanced way. In particular, the Council states, "The students should be accustomed to work properly at their own development. They are to be formed in strength of character, and, in general, they are to learn to esteem those virtues which are held in high regard by men and which

recommend a minister of Christ. Such virtues are sincerity of mind, a constant concern for justice, fidelity to one's promises, refinement in manners, modesty in speech coupled with charity." The passage makes explicit reference to Paul VI's apostolic letter, *Summi Dei Verbum*, published during the Council on November 4, 1963. The letter speaks of the cultivation of natural virtues and of the necessity of a human, Christian, and priestly formation, which must occur simultaneously. The theoretical reference point is taken from the *Prima Pars* of St. Thomas's *Summa*, which states, "*Cum enim gratia non tollat naturam sed perficiat. Oportet quod naturalis inclinatio subserviat fidei, sicut et naturalis inclinatio voluntatis obsequitur caritati*" (q. 1, a. 8). But the letter adds, "Still the importance of good qualities and human virtues cannot be overemphasized, as if the true and lasting success of the priestly ministry were eminently dependent on human resources; on the other hand, it is not possible to educate man to the natural virtues of prudence, justice, fortitude, temperance, humility, meekness etc. by exclusively referring to reason alone and to the methods of human sciences such as experimental psychology and pedagogy. It is fact the doctrine of the Catholic Church that without the healing grace of our Savior it is not possible to fulfill the commandments of the natural law and hence to acquire perfect virtue." From these words, we can draw an important conclusion: we are not to educate the man first, so that he might be Christian. Rather, we are to educate him in faith and charity because we find in these the fullness of humanity.

In the thirty years following Vatican Council II, the Roman congregations mentioned published various documents that took different aspects of seminary formation into consideration, treating them separately. Already on December 22, 1965, at the end of the Council, what was then called the Sacred Congregation for Seminaries and Universities published an instruction, *Doctrina et Exemplo*, dedicated to the liturgical formation of seminarians. Also noteworthy was the February 22, 1976 document of the Congregation for Catholic Education, *The Theological Formation of Future Priests*, as well as the January 6, 1980 English-language document of the same Congregation, *Spiritual Formation in Seminaries*. On January 6, 1970, the Congregation for Catholic Education published *Ratio Fundamentalis Istitutionis Sacerdotalis*, to which episcopal conferences were to refer when drafting their regulations. This document dealt at length with spiritual formation (nos. 44-58), and, within this (as in *Optatam Totius*), of the formation of all human gifts. Only after this come intellectual formation (nos. 59-64) through study (nos. 65-81) and pastoral formation (nos. 82-85). On April 11, 1974, the same Congregation published the Italian-language *Orientamenti educativi per la formazione al celibato sacerdotale*. This document

But human formation and Christian formation cannot be dealt with separately. In recent years, due to a renewed (and correct) emphasis on the priest as a "whole" human being, we have at times witnessed more of a search for the "perfect" man rather than for the "real" one. In 1970, *Ratio Fundamentalis* said that "even though the vocation to the priesthood is a supernatural gift and thus completely gratuitous, it necessarily rests on natural talents; so much so that if one of those talents is missing, one can well doubt of the existence of a true vocation" (no. 11). The 1974 *Orientamenti educativi per la formazione al celibato sacerdotale* [Educational guidelines for formation for the celibate priesthood] goes so far as to say, "If the man is not there, the call cannot be present" (no. 19).

---

looked at seminary education from a threefold perspective: "formation toward human maturity" (nos. 18-23); "formation toward Christian maturity" (nos. 24-28); and "formation toward priestly maturity (nos. 29-33).

We must affirm that while the human education of candidates for the priesthood has been a central theme, the accent has shifted over time: whereas documents published by the *Magisterium* in the years just after the Council put more emphasis on spiritual formation and on human formation within this, later documents took a more sectioned approach. *Pastores Dabo Vobis* in particular, after a discussion of the nature and mission of the priesthood, dedicates chapter 3 to the shape of the priest's spiritual life, and looks at all the aspects of his person and mission together. In chapter 5, however, when the document discusses the candidate's formation, it takes a more analytic perspective, identifying four parts: human formation (nos. 43-44); spiritual formation (nos. 45-50); intellectual formation (nos. 51-56); and pastoral formation (nos. 57-59); Human formation is necessary, we read in the text, "not only out of proper and due growth and realization of self, but also with a view to the ministry". For this latter, the candidates should "cultivate a series of human qualities.... needed for them to be balanced people, strong and free, capable of bearing the weight of pastoral responsibilities" (no. 43). Within this context, education in sexuality, freedom, and the moral conscience can be pursued (no. 44).

These are good observations, which, however, should not lead us to seek in the young candidate a perfect man. What we are to look for, rather, is a man who has really set out along a path, who seriously places the whole reality of his humanity, with all its gifts and shadows, at the feet of Christ. We look for a man who has not censured anything in himself, but who knows how to face self-sacrifice because he has already received the greatest treasure.

We must not be afraid to welcome people with lively, rich, or even problematic personalities into our seminaries and houses of formation, provided that they demonstrate clarity of intention, or, in the words of *Optatam Totius*, "proper intention and freedom of choice" (no. 6).

The candidate's experience at the seminary or house of formation should be one that does not stifle anything in the person's life, but rather, through right sacrifice, leads him to the fulfillment of every real expectation.

First of all, the seminary or house of formation should be the "home" of the experience of faith, of the experience of the People of God as the place in which promises are realized and the prophecy fulfilled. The call to be Christian received in Baptism is the primary condition for being a priest; the priest's active belonging to the people of God, the body of Christ, the holy nation, is a condition with respect to his specific sacramental function within this people.

In order to awaken in others an interest for Christ that coincides with a question about the reason for living, the priest must first be touched himself by the mysterious presence of Christ in his existence. He must be surprised by the irruption of Christ into his personal history and grateful for the encounters through which the Lord has shown and continues to show him his predilection, as well as his invitation to follow him as one of the baptized even before he is to follow him as an ordained minister.

Only a man who has discerned his priestly vocation on the basis of his experience of joy at being a Christian, a joy shared with others throughout his childhood, adolescence, and youth, can discover the humanly higher value contained in the Christian experience. When the priest lacks this experience, he will at most swell the ranks of already too many functionaries, all of whom are more or less intellectually prepared, more or less virtuous, "spiritual," or "moral," but incapable of radiating and proclaiming the only thing in Christianity that really interests people of every age: the fact that human life has a meaning at every instant; that it is possible to live totally; that happiness and the fullness of what is human can be reached through a relationship with the person of Christ, who is mysteriously but really present among us here and now through the communion of Christians.

This is also why it is right for seminaries and houses of formation to be structured so as to value and promote the desire of young people, whose vocations arose in the context of concrete ecclesial experiences, to keep up a living relationship with these particular Christian experiences.[71]

Before everything else that I have stressed, the greatest danger seems to me to be either forgetfulness of self or the desire to affirm the self at all costs. As to the first, the "losing oneself" demanded by Christ is not the same thing as a lack of interest in one's own "I," in a self-annihilation that has nothing to do with Christianity. We cannot forget that Christ said, "Whoever loses himself, finds himself" (Mk

---

[71] Cf. John Paul II, *Pastores Dabo Vobis*, no. 68.

8:35). He shows us that the end is the finding, the resurrection; the loss is the path. The second risk is a desire to affirm oneself which is incapable of sacrifice, incapable, that is, of recognizing that everything has already been given to us.

The Dangers of Spiritualism and Activism

There is another important point that must be considered in priestly formation: helping the young person to avoid the risks of spiritualism or activism. These seem to me to be the two greatest risks in which the life of the priest, as well as that of the whole Christian people, is immersed. Both of these risks are hidden beneath a loss of awareness of the nature of mission, and even of mission as the point of the priesthood and of the Christian life as such.

In an intervention in the October 19, 1993 plenary session of the Congregation for the Clergy, on the theme, "The Life, Ministry, and Permanent Formation of Priests,"[72] Fr. Giussani affirmed,

I have always thought that if someone had personally asked Christ, "What is your chief thought about yourself? What are you, in your eyes?" he would have responded, "I am the One Sent by the Father." To see one's own existence as mission. This is so true that, in creating the human place with which, through the Holy Spirit, he would set out on his paths into the

---

[72] L. Giussani, "Vita e Spirito del sacerdote cattolico," in 30 *Giorni*, (1993) 11, 37-44.

world, Christ spoke this word of generation: "As the Father has sent me, so I send you" (Jn 20:21; cf. Jn 13:20, 17:18).

If someone had met an apostle on a ship in the Mediterranean or along the Roman roads, and, upon hearing him speak, had asked him, "Who are you? Why are you here?," the all-encompassing answer would have been: "I am one sent by Jesus of Nazareth; I am one sent by Christ." ("Paul, called to be an apostle of Christ Jesus by the will of God" [1 Cor 1:1]. "Paul an apostle—sent neither by human commission nor from human autorities, but through Jesus Christ and God the Father, who raised him from the dead" [Gal 1:1; cf. 2 Cor 1:1; Eph 1:1; 1 Tim 1]).[73]

A society like ours can be touched only by the grace of a different kind of humanity, one marked by this new self-consciousness. I am sent so that, through my humanity, others may be reached by the One who has been sent by the Father. God became man because men and women can be touched only by the grace of a renewed humanity. This is true at all times, but it is especially true today, when society is suffocated at every turn by billions of words and messages, all of whose meaning is so relative that they have next to no meaning at all. *Christianity cannot renounce the truth of its origins; it cannot do without personal communication.* Everything can help, but nothing can replace personal communication.

Spiritualism and bureaucracy are opposing dangers that are in reality mirror images, and both hinder the

---

[73] *Ibid.*, 38-39.

development and carrying out of the Church's mission. The spiritualistic reduction sees Christianity solely in terms of an individual relationship with God, of the individual's spirit with God. It carries a risk of disincarnation that has its source in egoism and fear, and thus also in a lack of mercy for the human person and a deep forgetfulness of the reality of Christianity: God made man, God who bent down to save human beings. Spiritualism confines Christianity to a disincarnate prayer, to the silence of solipsism and an escape from the responsibilities of the present moment.

On the other hand, the activism favored by the growing bureaucratization of ecclesial life after the Second Vatican Council reduces the Christian life to meetings, conventions, and documents, to the business of "doing things for others" which nonetheless lacks the awareness and the responsibility of proclaiming Christ. What both errors are missing is the beauty of a life lived in communion here and now, the only experience on the basis of which a person can feel him or herself to be *sent* to the ends of the earth. The awareness of belonging to Christ is missing, as well as the experience, in the place where one has been called, of a belonging that sends one out.

Human freedom is activated in a human place. In his above-mentioned intervention, Fr. Giussani says,

To the freedom of Christ corresponds a freedom made available to him in those "called". Christ calls them "his own," and to them he sends his Spirit. Belonging to him is realized through this gift of the Spirit. Belonging to an Other is the complete definition of the essential condition of one's own personality; I am no longer my own. It is no longer conceivable to live for myself. I live for the other.[74]

We have forgotten the reality of the incarnation and the method it brought into the world. As Ratzinger says, "What is essential and fundamental for the priestly ministry is a deep personal relationship with Christ.... The priest must be a man who knows Jesus intimately, who has met him and learned to love him."[75] Referring to seminaries and houses of formation, Ratzinger elaborates on this theme of the house as "a community familiar with Jesus Christ."[76] The fundamental value of a Christian community lies in its "offering a space in which this spiritual edification can occur constantly,"[77] where the members accept "pruning", and it is possible to form real men and educate them in the truth.

My experience in the last years brings to mind three guidelines that can help the time spent at the seminary to be an authentic education in this dimension of mission.

a) Education in the Liturgy

In a certain sense, the liturgy holds first place in the education and formation of a seminarian, and does so in an enduring and ever-deeper way for the priest. The liturgy is an event which shapes life; it is the original source of our knowledge of Christ. In the liturgy, Christ gives himself to us and becomes a source of knowledge, in us and beyond us. This is true both of the sacraments and the Liturgy of the Hours. Because of this, it is not possible for a real striving after

---

[74] L. Giussani, "Vita e Spirito..." 40.

[75] J. Ratzinger, La Chiesa: Una communità sempre in cammino (Milano, 1991), 91.

[76] J. Ratzinger, "Prospettive della formazione...".

[77] Ibid.

Christ to neglect conscious participation in the liturgy as an experience of him, as the communication of his wisdom to us through a knowledge of the Old and New Testaments, as a prayer of Christ to Christ. The liturgy is the tremendous school of our being and knowledge. Educating a seminarian or priest in the liturgy does not at all mean cultivating a taste for some sort of liturgical aestheticism, or attempting to inject new interest into something that has begun to bore us through the arbitrariness of our words or gestures. Rather, it means educating a person in the essential form of the Christian life and its mission.

b) Education in Silence
We cannot remain before a Presence, before the person of Chirst present here and now, if we are not educated in silence. The hermit Laurentius commented, "Then I understood that my life would be spent in the memory of what had happened to me. And the memory of you fills me with silence." Our knowledge of Christ is *donum Dei altissimi*, the gift of the Most High God, and so we must beg for it with tenacity and faithfulness.

For this reason, a time of the day systematically dedicated to silence is fundamental to the life of a priest. Without it, his life goes up in smoke, dispersed among a million details and preoccupations. The life of a priest, even the most active missionary, must have, deep down, a monastic structure, otherwise it will remain fragile and incapable of real construction. It is in silence that one learns to be with people in a different way, to speak to them or laugh with them differently. One becomes more joyful and more profound at the same time.

Silence must not be reduced to "catch-up time." Even if it is set aside for reading—the lives of the saints or Church history—it has to have the structure of prayer. For this reason, I tell my seminarians that we are to begin the daily hour of silence in our house of formation with ten minutes of praying on our knees, in front of Christ, and to end it with a decade of the rosary, a prayer that is an entreaty to God, offering ourselves to him, invoking his blessing on the Church and on persons entrusted to us. Only a reason of pressing charity should dispense us from this time of the day given directly to Christ.

c) *Education in Gratuity*[78]

Gratuity is the dimension of the priest's very being, because it is the dimension of the new creature, the Christian. An education in this dimension is more necessary than ever today, when the prevailing mentality holds up lying in the face of reality as the only possible human position. This mentality is one of the opposite of gratuity: consumption. Reality external to the self, every "thou," be it a person or a thing, is seen by the prevailing mentality—which then imposes itself on us—as something we can help ourselves to, something to use up or out of which we can extract an immediate usefulness. They are no longer things we might open ourselves to, welcome, listen to, or make blossom from within.

The question of the person's position in the face of being is a fundamental one for every human being, but it takes on an extraordinary importance for those of us called to be educators. We are called to live in relationship with other people whom we must help to reach this position of

---

[78] Gratuity's Latin root *gratuias/gratas* is the translation of the Greek *charis*, that English translates as *charity*.

truth. What could we say, what could we bring to others, if we did not live out this gratuity ourselves?

The possibility of a common life—for all who are called to live it, which includes everyone in the seminary—is closely linked to an education in gratuity, because there can be no common life if there is no welcome extended to the other for who he is, and not for what he gives. The fundamental question of freedom from the fruit of one's own labor is also closely linked to an education in gratuity.

We are creatures made by God, beings who have received being. Our being is by nature dependent, open, and listening. An education in gratuity is aimed at finding this original position again. Concretely, how can it be carried out? Through a block of time during the week systematically dedicated to a relationship with others, whoever they may be, for the sole reason that they *are*. This helps us to attune our hearts and minds to the perception of the Absolute Gratuity who makes all things, persons, and the world, a gratuity we come from and go toward, and in which everything consists.

This time, be it a little or a lot, regularly spent on self-education, is an education in a permanent dimension of life. When lived in a real way, it tends to influence how we form relationships with others. It also influences our silence, because deep down they have the same root: both are an act of prayer.

Love for the Truth

The priest must be able to give an account of his faith better than others; he must know how to show in his own experience how the following of Christ changes one's life.

Ratzinger observes that the task of proclamation proper to a priest does not require a telegraph operator, but a witness. The priest must refer to the words of another in the first person, in a way that is completely personal, immersing himself in them so fully that they become his: "In this process, in which one introduces oneself to, understands, penetrates, and lives within this Word, lies the essence of every priestly formation."[79]

During this formation, study should not be reduced to the accumulation of knowledge. The Latin word *studium* implies, even before an idea of knowledge, an application of the whole person, so that what is encountered in study might reach its fullest dimensions. Study has as its aim "that they may know you, the only true God, and Jesus Christ whom you have sent" (Jn 17:3). In the life of a young man called to the priesthood, this does not begin from nothing; it begins with the event of faith, which first happened to him when he became a Christian. It is *fides quaerens intellectum*, the experience of faith seeking understanding. It is a penetration of that Event, an understanding and penetration of the "I", which reaches its mysterious origin. As St. Augustine declares at the beginning of his *Soliloquies*, "*Deum et animam nihil amplius.*"

This point is of fundamental importance in an education in study, so that faith might be the beginning and the end of the intellectual formation of the young. In this way, their knowledge will be able to overflow into the unity of faith, into that unitary vision contained in the life of faith. Ratzinger continues:

---

[79] J. Ratzinger, "*Prospettive della formazione...*".

It seems to me that today, in an age of increasing specialization, there is an urgent need to preserve theology's internal unity and concentric unfolding from an essential core. Of course, a theologian ought to possess a high degree of culture. However, theology must also be able to throw off excess weight and concentrate on the essential. When so-called "specialized study" leads to the accumulation of unrelated pieces of knowledge, it has not performed its task. Only in a vision of the whole do the criteria necessary for a discernment of spirits and for the spiritual independence of the one proclaiming also take become apparent. If the theologian does not learn to judge from the point of view of the whole, he remains defenseless, at the mercy of changing fashions.[80]

In order for the priest to be a communicator of truth, he cannot possess it as some kind of analytical baggage, but as something that has renewed his life. He bears witness to a truth from which he lives. The communication of truth in the Church is always a communication of grace, person to person, heart to heart.

The Priest as Creator of a People

Our society has lost the idea of the person, and thus cannot experience what it means to be a people. A people is made up of persons moved by a common experience. The

---

[80] Ibid.

fascinating adventure the Christian finds him or herself facing today—which the priest, as a Christian, is called to share in and sustain—is that of the reconstruction of a people. This is an adventure in which we are called to take again the same steps taken at the Church's beginning. The self-perception of today's Christian community cannot be much different from that of the tiny community of Rome or the larger one at Corinth in the times of St. Paul; they must have seen themselves lost in the immensity of an empire.

For this task, teaching people to remember the Mother of God is of the utmost importance, because she kept in her heart what we are also called to keep: the assurance that this man living among us and through us is the meaning of the world and history. Oftentimes Christians are no longer conscious of being the "remnant of Israel." Our hurry to insert ourselves into the world has caused us to forget the meaning of "facing" the world, with the responsibility of bringing it something that others do not have and do not know.

This can serve as a summary of what I have briefly tried to explain in this chapter: educators, in order to be such, must be conscious of the gift they have received, as well as of the responsibility with regard to both God and their fellow human beings, which is the Christian vocation. This consciousness is born and continually reborn through the miracles that Christ never allows to be lacking in his Church. For this reason, I have spoken of the experience of a changed humanity that, in the power of the proclamation and the regeneration effected by the sacraments, gathers a people around it.

Liturgy, silence, the experience of gratuity, and study understood as a deepening of faith, seem to me to be the fundamental steps in the education of a young seminarian, forming him for the task of guiding the community.

Afterword

I would like to thank Msgr. Massimo Camisasca for this small book in which, through some significant moments of its brief history, he describes the essential characteristics of the Priestly Fraternity of the Missionaries of St. Charles Borromeo and offers some of his reflections on priestly formation.

As the author writes, this Priestly Fraternity is one of the "unforeseen and unintended" fruits God has granted in the history of our Movement: Communion and Liberation. Who would have thought that, from the original group of five priests from the "Paradiso" missionary community in Bergamo, who moved to Rome in 1985, this "company of adventurers" would arise under the guidance of Msgr. Camisasca, numbering more than ninety priests in fourteen countries around the world, as well as a large group of seminarians in the house of formation?

I see the Fraternity as the most important work in the history of our movement. First, because it lives out the aim, formally expressed in its statutes, of bringing the content and experience of Communion and Liberation into the whole world. Second, because a stream of people called to participate in an authentic, intelligent, and passionate way in the mystery of Christ's priesthood ensures the education *"forma gregis ex animo"* that makes the leaders of the People of God into a more effective witnesses.

Reading these pages, I was struck by the continual resurfacing of an intuition that has accompanied me from the very beginning of the *Gioventù Studentesca*, which I have repeated in the many occasions I have had to speak to priests. It begins with a question: What is the first condition for bringing Christ to others? Being a real man or a real woman. Bringing Christ to others implies bearing witness to them that, in my experience, he responds to my humanity: Christ is the response to the needs of our humanity.

For the priest, a lived belonging to Christ as the One Sent by the Father (cf. Jn 20:21) is the exhaustive definition of his own personality (cf. Gal 2:20). "[The priest's] life and ministry"—I said in a communiqué of the 1995 international symposium of the Congregation for the Clergy in Rome—"are thus a response to a real, historical, and existential Event; he is consumed by the love of Christ, crucified and risen (cf. 2 Cor 5:14ff)." This consuming love makes us participate in the mission for which he came, died, and rose again: that everyone who lives no longer lives for himself, but for him who died and was raised for them. This urgency of Christ's love, that ensures the memory of God's love for human person, is the goal toward which all our desire and all our activity tend.

It is my hope that the Fraternity grows in numbers, but above all in truth. That is, I hope that it becomes more and more aware of the reason why it was born and keeps itself true in all its freshness as well. May its priests be real men. Through what they say and especially through their persons, may they know how to proclaim Christ, the redeemer of the human person, to others.

I express my gratitude to Msgr. Camisasca for his long friendship and for the responsibility as father and guide that he took on when founding the Fraternity. I thus consider him totally, deeply, and intensely in communion with the experience that springs from the charism of Communion and Liberation.

Luigi Giussani
Founder of Communion and Liberation

About The Author

Massimo Camisasca is the Superior General of the Priestly Fraternity of the Missionaries of St. Charles Borromeo. Formerly a professor of metaphysics at the Lateran University and the John Paul II Institute in Rome, Camisasca has been involved in priestly formation for the last twenty-five years. His many books published in Italian include "Communion and Liberation" (3 vols.), "Don Giussani. La sua esperienza di Dio e dell'uomo", "Padre. Ci saranno ancora sacerdoti nel futuro della Chiesa?". In English, "The Challenge of Fatherood" is also available .

www.fraternityofsaintcharles.org

CPSIA information can be obtained
at www.ICGtesting.com
Printed in the USA
BVHW082106040321
601611BV00008B/880